Information for Yorkshire Genealogists

History, Archives, Journals, etc.

Stuart A. Raymond

Yorkshire: The Genealogists Library Guide 1

Published by the
Federation of Family History Societies (Publications) Ltd.,
Units 15-16 Chesham Industrial Estate
Oram Street, Bury
Lancashire, BL9 6EN, UK

Copies also obtainable from:
S.A. & M.J. Raymond
P.O.Box 35, Exeter, Devon, EX1 3YZ, U.K.
Email: stuart@samjraymond.softnet.co.uk
http://www.soft.net.uk/samjraymond/igb.htm

First published 2000

ISBN: 1 86006 118 4 (FFHS (Publications) Ltd)

ISBN: 1 899668 13 6 (S.A. & M.J. Raymond)

ISSN: 1033-2065

Printed and bound by the Alden Group, London and Northampton.

Contents

Front cover: York Minster

Introduction

This guide to published sources of genealogical information is intended primarily for genealogists. It is, however, hoped that it will also prove useful to historians, librarians, archivists, research students, and anyone else interested in the history of Yorkshire. It is intended to be used in conjunction with my *English genealogy: an introductory bibliography,* with the other volumes of *Yorkshire: the genealogists library guide,* and the companion volumes in the *British genealogical library guides* series. A full list of these volumes appears on the back cover.

Many genealogists, when they begin their research, do not realise just how much information has been published, and is readily available in printed form. Not infrequently, they head straight for the archives, rather than checking printed sources first. In so doing, they waste much time, and also impose needless wear and tear on irreplaceable archives. However, when faced with the vast array of tomes possessed by major reference libraries, it is difficult to know where to begin without guidance. This bibliography is intended to point you in the right direction. My aim has been to list everything relating to Yorkshire that has been published and is likely to be of use to genealogists. However, anyone who tries to compile a totally comprehensive bibliography of Yorkshire is likely to fall short of his aim. The task is almost impossible, especially if the endeavour is made by one person. That does not, however, mean that the attempt should not be made. Usefulness, rather than comprehensiveness, has been my prime aim - and this book would not be useful to anyone if its publication were to be prevented by a vain attempt to ensure total comprehensiveness. I am well aware that there are likely to be omissions, especially in view of the fact that, given constraints of time and money, it has not been possible for me to visit all of the large number of libraries with substantial collections on Yorkshire's history. Each of them may well possess works not held anywhere else. The identification of such works is not, however, a major aim of this bibliography. Rather, my purpose has been to enable you to identify works which are mostly readily available. Some titles you may be able to purchase; all can be found in libraries throughout the English-speaking world. You can check the holdings of many libraries via their catalogues on the internet; alternatively, if your local library does not hold a particular book, the librarian should be able to tell you where to find it — and, as a last resort, may be able to borrow it for you via the inter-library loan network, irrespective of whether you live in London or San Francisco. Many overseas libraries have good collections of books on English genealogy and local history, for example, several of the Australian state libraries. The libraries of family history societies are also worth checking — even if they are far distant from Yorkshire: for example, the Genealogical Society of Victoria, in Melbourne, has a good collection of books on English genealogy. Some family history societies offer a postal borrowing service; others may be willing to check a particular book for you. It is also worth joining one of the genealogical newsgroups or mailing lists on the internet; other members may hold the books you need, and be willing to check them for you.

In general, I have not included works which are national in scope but which have local content. Many such works may be identified in *English genealogy: a bibliography,* to which reference is made at appropriate points below. The innumerable notes and queries to be found in family history society journals etc., are excluded, except where their content is of importance. Where I have included such notes, replies to them are cited in the form 'see also', with no reference to the names of respondents. I have also excluded extracts from newspapers, and histories which have not been published. Where possible, citations are accompanied by notes indicating the period covered, the locality/ies concerned, and other pertinent information. Most of the items listed here have been physically examined to ensure that they are relevant, and that correct bibliographical details are given. However, a few items have proved elusive, and yet worthy of mention; these are noted 'not seen', and I cannot guarantee the accuracy of the information provided in these entries.

For Yorkshire, so much information has been published that no less than 6 volumes are required to list relevant citations. This volume identifies a wide range of background information. Every genealogist needs to know something about the history of the area his or her ancestors came from, and so the first two sections of this volume are devoted to the listing of historical studies of the county and its localities — many of which contain valuable genealogical information. These sections are far from being comprehensive, since they concentrate on those works most likely to be of use to genealogists. There follow sections dealing with the wide range of library resources and archival repositories that are available, the numerous journals, and the various family history societies. Place-names, maps and migration are dealt with in the final sections.

Four further volumes of *Yorkshire: the genealogists library guide* list the wide range of published sources that are available; the final volume lists innumerable published family histories and pedigrees. These volumes may also include information relevant to the contents of this volume, not repeated here.

Be warned: just because information has been published, it does not necessarily follow that it is accurate. I have not made any judgement on the accuracy of most works listed: that is up to you.

If you are an assiduous researcher, you may well come across items I have missed. If you do, please let me know, so that they can be included in the next edition.

The work of compiling this bibliography has depended heavily on the resources of the libraries I have used. These included the local studies collections in the public libraries of Bradford, Doncaster, Hull, Leeds, Sheffield, and York, the Brotherton Library at the University of Leeds, the British Library, the Society of Genealogists, Guildhall Library, the University and the Central Library in Bristol, the University of Exeter library and the Exeter Public Library in Exeter. I have also used the resources of a number of family history societies, and am particularly grateful to the societies for Devon, Cornwall, Somerset & Dorset, Sheffield and Ripon/Harrogate. All these institutions deserve my thanks, as does John Perkins, who read and commented on an early draft of the book. Mary Raymond typed the manuscript, Mark Gant undertook most of the indexing, and Bob Boyd saw the book through the press. I am grateful too to the officers of the Federation of Family History Societies, whose support is vital for the continuation of this series. My thanks also to my wife Marjorie.

Stuart A. Raymond

Abbreviations

B.A.	*Bradford antiquary*
B.I.B.	*Borthwick Institute bulletin*
B.S.H.S.	*Bulletin of the Saddleworth Historical Society*
B.T.C.	Borthwick texts and calendars: records of the Northen Provinces
Bk.I.H.R	*Borthwick Institute of Historical Research*
B.T.	*Banyan tree: journal of the East Yorkshire Family History Society.*
C.T.L.H.S.B.	*Cleveland and Teeside Local History Society bulletin*
C.Y.D.F.H.S.J.	*City of York & District Family History Society Journal*
Don. Anc.	*Doncaster Ancestor*
E.Y.F.H.S.	East Yorkshire Family History Society
E.Y.L.H.S.	East Yorkshire Local History Society series
F.H.S.	Family History Society
F.S.	*Flowing stream: journal of Sheffield & District Family History Society*
H. & D.F.H.S.	Huddersfield & District Family History Society
H. & D.F.H.S.J.	*Huddersfield & District Family History Society journal*
J.Cl.F.H.S.	*Journal of the Cleveland Family History Society*
K.D.F.H.S.J.	*Keighley & District Family History Society journal.*
N.H.	*Northern history*
N.Y.C.R.O.P.	North Yorkshire County Record Office publications
O.W.R.	*Old West Riding*
P.R.H.A.S.	*Papers, reports, etc., read before the Halifax Antiquarian Society*
R. & D.F.H.S.N.	*Rotherham and District Family History Society newsletter*
R.H.	*Ripon Historian*
T.E.R.A.S.	*Transactions of the East Riding Archaeological Society*
T. Hal. A.S.	*Transactions of the Halifax Archaeological Society*
T. Hunter A.S.	*Transactions of the Hunter Archaeological Society*
T.S.	Thoresby Society

Wh.N.	*Wharfedale newsletter: the journal of the Wharfedale Family History Group.*
Y.A.J.	*Yorkshire archaeological journal*
Y.A.S.,	F.H.P.S.S. Yorkshire Archaeological Society. Family History and Population Studies Section
Y.A.S., F.H.P.S.S.N.	*Yorkshire Archaeological Society. Family History and Population Studies Section newsletter*
Y.A.S., P.R.S.	Yorkshire Archaeological Society. Parish Register Section
Y.A.S., R.S.	Yorkshire Archaeological Society. Record Series
Y.C.M.	*Yorkshire county magazine*
Y.F.H.	*Yorkshire family historian*
Y.F.H.S.N.	*York Family History Society newsletter*
Y.G.	*Yorkshire genealogist*
Y.N.Q. II.	*Yorkshire notes & queries* [1905-9]

Bibliographic Presentation

Authors names are in SMALL CAPITALS. Book and journal titles are in *italics*. Articles appearing in journals, and material such as parish register transcripts, forming only part of books are in inverted commas and textface type. Volume numbers are in **bold** and the individual number of the journal may be shown in parentheses. These are normally followed by the place of publication (except where this is London, which is omitted), the name of the publisher and the date of publication. In the case of articles, further figures indicate page numbers.

Libraries

Many libraries have substantial collections of books and journals on Yorkshire history; only a select list of addresses can be given here. I have not included the addresses of most family history societies, whose libraries are available to their members, and which ought to be used by everyone tracing their ancestors in the area covered. Their addresses change frequently, and any listing would be out of date by the time it was printed. Current addresses are regularly published in *Family history news & digest.*

I have also excluded the addresses of most Yorkshire record repositories. These hold the archives you may need to consult, but generally speaking do not have large collections of printed books.

It is also worth pointing out that many public and university libraries throughout the English-speaking world hold much Yorkshire material; in particular, many university libraries subscribe to major series such as the *Yorkshire archaeological journal* and the Yorkshire Archaeological Society's *Record series* - which may also be available in the libraries of the major county historical societies who exchange journals with them.

Major collections of Yorkshire material are to be found in at least two London institutions:

British Library
96, Euston Road,
London,
NW1 2DB

Society of Genealogists,
14, Charterhouse Buildings,
Goswell Road,
London,
EC1M 7BA

The two Yorkshire institutions with a county-wide remit are:

Borthwick Institute,
University of York,
St.Anthony's Hall
Peasholme Green,
York,
YO1 2PW

Yorkshire Archaeological Society
Claremont,
23, Clarendon Road,
Leeds,
LS2 9NZ

A number of university libraries in the county have important Yorkshire collections:

Brynmor Jones Library,
University of Hull,
Hull, HU6 7RX
(Houses the East Yorkshire Bibliography)

Brotherton Library
University of Leeds
Leeds, LS2 9JT

The major local collections in public libraries are:

Bradford
Bradford Central Library
Princes Way,
Bradford,
BD1 1NN

Hull
Local Studies Library,
Hull Central Library
Albion Street,
Hull, HU1 3TF

Leeds
Local History Collection,
Central Library,
Calverley Street.
Leeds, LS1 3AB

Middlesbrough
Local Collection,
Middlesbrough Reference Library,
Victoria Square,
Middlesbrough,
Cleveland,
TS1 2AY

Sheffield
Local Studies Library,
Sheffield City Libraries,
Surrey Street,
Sheffield, S1 1XZ

York
York City Library,
Reference Library,
Local Studies Collection,
Museum Street,
York, YO1 2DS

1. THE HISTORY OF YORKSHIRE

In order to understand the histories of our families, it is essential to have some appreciation of the society in which they lived, and some knowledge of the historical background. There are numerous historical studies of Yorkshire, and the listing which follows is selective. A good modern introduction is provided by:

RAWNSLEY, S.J., & SINGLETON, F.B. *A history of Yorkshire*. 3rd ed. Darwen county history series. Chichester: Phillimore & Co., 1995.

The standard series of English county histories is the *Victoria county history*. The volumes for the East Riding (see below) and York (see section 2 below) are particularly valuable, providing surveys of the history of numerous individual parishes. The general volumes for Yorkshire may also prove useful:

PAGE, WILLIAM. *The Victoria history of the county of York*. 3 vols. Archibald Constable and Company, 1907. v.2 includes a transcript of Domesday Book.

A number of substantial county histories were published in the nineteenth century. These included:

ALLEN, THOMAS. *A new and complete history of the County of York*. 6 vols. I.T. Hinton, 1829-31. Parochial survey.

BAINES, THOMAS. *Yorkshire past and present: a history and description of the three ridings of the great County of York, from the earliest ages to the year 1870, with an account of its manufactures, commerce and civil and mechanical engineering ...* 2 vols. in 3. William Mackenzie, [1871-77].

BIGLAND, JOHN. *A topographical and historical description of the County of York, containing an account of its towns, antiquities, public edifices, cathedral, churches, picturesque scenery, castles, monuments, scenery, the residences of the nobility, gentry, &c., accompanied with biographical notices of eminent and learned men to whom this county has given birth*. Sherwood, Neely and Jones, 1812. Re-issue of the *Beauties of England, 12*.

FLETCHER, J.S. *Picturesque history of Yorkshire, being an account of the history, topography, antiquities, industries and modern life of the cities, towns and villages of the County of York, founded on personal observations made during many journeys through the three ridings*. 6 vols. Caxton Publishing Co., [18--]. Extensive.

The modern approach to county history is exemplified in:

HEY, DAVID. *Yorkshire from A.D.1000*. Regional history of England series. Longman, 1986.

There are many studies of specific periods and topics; those covering the whole county are listed here in rough chronological order. Studies dealing with specific Ridings (the ancient divisions of the county) follow, and in section 2 local and parochial histories are listed. Volumes of parochial surveys are particularly useful, since these frequently contain numerous monumental inscriptions, pedigrees, and extracts from genealogical sources. It should be noted that the area now known as 'South Yorkshire' was part of the West Riding until 1974.

Medieval Period

STENTON, FRANK MERRY. *Type of manorial structure in the northern Danelaw*. Oxford studies in social and legal history 7. Oxford: Clarendon Press, 1910. Study of Yorkshire, Derbyshire, Nottinghamshire, Leicestershire, Lincolnshire and Rutland, 10-12th c.

KAPELLE, WILLIAM E. *The Norman conquest of the North: the region and its transformation, 1000-1135*. Croom Helm, 1979.

DALTON, PAUL. *Conquest, anarchy and lordship: Yorkshire, 1066-1154*. Cambridge studies in medieval life and thought, 4th series 27. Cambridge: Cambridge University Press, 1994.

LE PATOUREL, JOHN. 'The Norman Conquest of Yorkshire', *N.H.* 6, 1971, 1-21.

BISHOP, T.A.M. 'The Norman settlement of Yorkshire', in HUNT, R.W., PANTIN, W.A., & SOUTHERN, R.W., eds. *Studies in medieval history presented to F.M. Powicke*. Oxford: Clarendon Press, 1948, 1-14.

THOMAS, HUGH M. *Vassals, heiresses, crusaders and thugs: the gentry of Angevin Yorkshire, 1154-1216.* Philadelphia: University of Pennsylvania Press, 1993.

HUGHES, JONATHAN. *Pastors and visionaries: religion and secular life in late medieval Yorkshire.* Woodbridge: Boydell Press, 1988. Based on Yorkshire devotional literature, c.1350-1450.

VALE, M.G.A. *Piety, charity and literacy amongy the Yorkshire gentry, 1370-1480.* Borthwick papers 50. 1976. Based on wills.

GOLDBERG, P.J.P. *Women, work and life cycle in a medieval economy: women in York and Yorkshire, c.1300-1520.* Oxford: Clarendon Press, 1992. Study of economic opportunity and marriage amongst women in York and Yorkshire, 14-15th c., based on York civic records, probate records, poll tax returns, *etc.*

GOLDBERG, P.J.P. 'Womens work, womens rule, in the late medieval north', in HICKS, MICHAEL, ed. *Profit, piety and the professions in later medieval England.* Gloucester: Alan Sutton, 1990, 34-50. Based on poll tax returns, 1379, for the West Riding and Howdenshire.

GOLDBERG, P.J.P. 'Marriage, migration, servanthood and life-cycle in Yorkshire towns of the later middle ages: some York cause paper evidence', *Continuity and change* 1(2), 1986, 141-69. Based on ecclesiastical court records.

DOBSON, R.B. 'The risings in York, Beverley and Scarborough, 1380-1381', in HILTON, R.H., & ASTON, T.H., eds. *The English rising of 1381.* Cambridge: Cambridge University Press, 1984, 112-42.

POLLARD, A.J. *North-Eastern England during the Wars of the Roses: lay society, war and politics, 1450-1500.* Oxford: Clarendon Press, 1990. Scholarly study of Yorkshire, Northumberland and Co. Durham.

JORDAN, W.K. *The charities of rural England, 1480-1660: the aspirations and achievements of the rural society.* George Allen & Unwin, 1961. Based on wills of Buckinghamshire, Norfolk and Yorkshire.

Early Modern Period, 1500-1800

HICKS, M.A. 'The Yorkshire rebellion of 1489 reconsidered', *N.H.* **22**, 1986, 39-62.

CLIFFE, J.T. *The Yorkshire gentry: from the Reformation to the Civil War.* Athlone Press, 1969.

BUSH, M.L. 'The Richmondshire uprising of October 1536 and the Pilgrimage of Grace', *N.H.* **29**, 1993, 64-98.

CARTWRIGHT, J.J. *Chapters in the history of Yorkshire, being a collection of original letters, papers and public documents illustrating the state of that county in the reigns of Elizabeth, James I and Charles I.* Wakefield: B.W. Allen, 1872. Includes many interesting documents, especially relating to Sir Thomas Gargrave, Sir Martin Frobisher, *etc.*

ROEBUCK, PETER. *Yorkshire baronets, 1640-1750: families, estates and fortunes.* Oxford: Oxford University Press, 1980. Study of the Hotham, Beaumont, Constable, and Bright families, and their estates; includes pedigrees.

SCOTT, DAVID. 'Hannibal at our gates: loyalists and fifth-columnists during the Bishops' Wars – the case of Yorkshire', *Historical research* **70**(173), 1997, 269-93.

BENNETT, RONAN. 'War and disorder: policing the soldiery in civil war Yorkshire', in FISSEL, MARK CHARLES, ed. *War and government in Britain 1598-1650.* Manchester: Manchester University Press, 1991, 248-73. Based on Quarter Sessions records and assize files, *etc.*

HUDSON, PAT. 'Land, the social structure and industry in two Yorkshire townships c.1660-1800', in SWAN, PHILIP, & FOSTER, DAVID, eds. *Essays in regional and local history: in honour of Eric M. Sigsworth.* Cherry Barton: Hutton, 1992, 27-46.

PICKLES, MAY F. 'Labour migration: Yorkshire c.1670 to 1743', *Local population studies* **57**, 1996, 30-49. Based on hearth tax assessments, 1670s, and archiepiscopal visitation records 1743.

MCCUTCHEON, K.L. *Yorkshire fairs and markets to the end of the eighteenth century.* T.S. **39**. 1940.

WELLS, ROGER A.E. *Death and distress in Yorkshire, 1793-1802.* Borthwick papers 52. 1977.

19-20th centuries

BENSON, J., & NEVILLE, R.G. *Studies in the Yorkshire coal industry.* Manchester: Manchester University Press, 1976.

DINWIDDY, J.R. 'The 'black lamp' in Yorkshire, 1801-1802', *Past and present* **64**, 1974. 113-23. See also 124-35. Study of the 'revolutionary' tradition.

REID, ROBERT. *Land of lost content: the Luddite revolt, 1812.* Heinemann, 1986.

GREEN, S.J.D. *Religion in the age of decline: organisation and experience in industrial Yorkshire, 1870-1920.* Cambridge: Cambridge University Press, 1996.

JOWITT, J.A., ed. *Model industrial communities in mid-nineteenth century Yorkshire.* Bradford: University of Bradford, 1986. Includes general studies of Saltaire, Wilshaw, Meltham Mills, Keighley, *etc.*

East Riding

ALLISON, K.J. *A history of the County of York, East Riding.* 6 vols to date. Oxford University Press for the Institute of Historical Research, 1969-89. v.1. The city of Kingston upon Hull. v.2. [Dickering Wapentake]. v.3. [Ouse and Derwent Wapentake; Harthill Wapentake; Wilton Beacon Division]. v.4. [Harthill Wapentake, Hunsley Beacon Division]. v.5. Holderness: southern part. v.6. The borough and liberties of Beverley.

SHEAHAN, J.J., & WHELLAN, T. *History and topography of the City of York, the Ainsty Wapentake, and the East Riding of Yorkshire, embracing a general review of the early history of Great Britain, and a general history and description of the County of York.* 2 vols. Beverley: John Green, 1855-6. Parochial survey.

WOODWARD, DONALD, ed. *Descriptions of East Yorkshire: Leland to Defoe.* E.Y.L.H.S. **39**. 1985. Topographical accounts.

CROWTHER, JAN. *Descriptions of East Yorkshire: De La Pryme to Heard.* E.Y.L.H.S. **45**. 1992.

ALLISON, K.J. *The East Riding of Yorkshire landscape.* The making of the English landscape. Hodder and Stoughton, 1976.

BAKER. W.P. *Parish registers and illiteracy in East Yorkshire.* E.Y.L.H.S. **13**. 1961. Discussion of the historical use of parish registers.

ENGLISH, BARBARA. *The great landowners of East Yorkshire, 1530-1910.* Hemel Hempstead: Harvester Wheatsheaf, 1990. Study of major estates.

ENGLISH, BARBARA. 'Patterns of estate management in East Yorkshire c.1840-c.1880', *Agricultural history review* **32**, 1984, 29-48. General study of estate management, identifying the major landowners.

HARRIS, ALAN. *The rural landscape of the East Riding of Yorkshire, 1700-1850: a study in historical geography.* Oxford: Oxford University Press, 1961. Reprinted Wakefield: S.R. Publishers, 1969.

HARRIS, ALAN. *The open fields of East Yorkshire.* E.Y.L.H.S. **9**. 1959. 18th c.

WARD, J.T. *East Yorkshire landed estates in the nineteenth century.* E.Y.L.H.S. **23**. 1967. Includes a list of principal landowners in 1875.

WILKINSON, OLGA. *The agricultural revolution in the East Riding of Yorkshire.* E.Y.L.H.S. **5**. 1964. General account.

NEAVE, DAVID. *Mutual aid in the Victorian countryside: friendly societies in the rural East Riding, 1830-1914.* Hull: Hull University Press, 1990. Interesting study of a neglected topic.

NEAVE, DAVID. *East Riding Friendly Societies.* E.Y.L.H.S. **41**. 1988. Includes list.

North Riding

WHELLAN, C., & CO. *History and topography of the City of York and the North Riding of Yorkshire, embracing a general review of the early history of Great Britain and a general history and description of the County of York.* 2 vols. Beverley: C. Whellan & Co., 1857. Parochial survey; many notes on descents *etc.*

Houses of the North York moors. H.M.S.O., 1987.

HARRISON, BARRY, & HUTTON, BARBARA. *Vernacular houses in North Yorkshire and Cleveland.* Edinburgh: John Donald, 1984. Architectural study; few names.

EDWARDS, WILLIAM. *The early history of the North Riding.* A. Brown and Sons, 1924. Medieval; includes chapter on 'Early Yorkshire pedigrees', with notes on baronial families.

HASTINGS, R.P. *Essays in North Riding history, 1780-1850.* N.Y.C.R.O.P., **28.** 1981.

West Riding

West Yorkshire: an archaeological survey to A.D. 1500. 3 vols. Wakefield: West Yorkshire Metropolitan County Council, 1981. Authoritative survey.

Parishes covered by Pontefract & District Family History Society. Pontefract: the Society, [1999?] Brief description of parishes and townships from Baines *directory,* 1823.

BRISCOE, GILL. *Pontefract and Wakefield ancestors: a family historians guide to sources and where to find them.* Pontefract: Pontefract & District F.H.S., [1999?]

RAISTRICK, ARTHUR. *West Riding of Yorkshire.* The making of the English landscape. Hodder and Stoughton, 1970.

HEY, DAVID. *The making of South Yorkshire.* Ashbourne: Moorland Publishing, 1979. To the 17th c.

PARSONS, EDWARD. *The civil, ecclesiastical, literary, commercial and miscellaneous history of Leeds, Halifax, Huddersfield, Bradford, Wakefield, Dewsbury, Otley, and the manufacturing district of Yorkshire.* 2 vols. Leeds: Frederick Hobson, 1834.

POLLARD, SIDNEY, & HULMES, COLIN. *Essays in the economic and social history of South Yorkshire.* Barnsley: South Yorkshire County Council, Recreation Culture and Health Department, 1976. Scholarly.

GILES, COLUM. *Rural houses of West Yorkshire, 1400-1830.* Royal Commission on Historical Monuments supplementary series **8.** H.M.S.O., 1986.

HEY, DAVID. *Packmen, carriers and packhorse roads: trade and communications in north Derbyshire and South Yorkshire.* [Leicester]: Leicester University Press, 1980.

SMITH, R.B. *Land and politics in the England of Henry VIII: the West Riding of Yorkshire, 1530-46.* Oxford: Clarendon Press, 1970.

ELY, JAMES W. The eighteenth-century poor laws in the West Riding of Yorkshire', *American journal of legal history* **30**(1), 1986, 1-24.

CAFFYN, LUCY. *Workers housing in West Yorkshire, 1750-1920.* Royal Commission on Historical Monuments supplementary series **9.** H.M.S.O., 1986.

HUDSON, PAT. *The genesis of industrial capital: a study of the West Riding wool textile industry, c.1750-1850.* Cambridge: Cambridge University Press, 1986. Includes useful list of sources.

SHEERAN, GEORGE. *Brass castles: West Yorkshire new rich and their houses, 1800-1914.* Halifax: Ryburn Publishing, 1993.

SMITH, LEONARD. *Religion and the rise of labour: nonconformity and the independent labour movement in Lancashire and the West Riding, 1880-1914.* Keele: Ryburn Publishing, 1994. Includes brief biographies of leading figures.

2. PARISH and LOCAL HISTORIES.

A comprehensive listing of Yorkshire parish and local histories would occupy an entire volume; the list which follows is selective. It aims to highlight older works containing many pedigrees and extracts from genealogical sources, modern studies based on sources used by genealogists, and some of the more important works of local historians. Where there are several works listed on a particular place, general studies are listed first, followed by a chronological itemisation of works on particular periods.

Ackworth
GREEN, W.A. *Historical antiquities of Ackworth from manor records and other sources, with lists of tenants and residents from the earliest times, of lords of the manor, incumbents, and chantrey priests.* Chiswick Press, 1910.

SAYWELL, J.L. *The parochial history of Ackworth, Yorks., with archaeological, antiquarian and biographical notes and records.* Pontefract: James Atkinson & Son, 1894.

Acomb
BENSON, G. 'Notes on Acomb, York', *Reports and papers of the Associated Architectural Societies* **38**, 1926, 72-94. Includes pedigrees of Acomb, 16-17th c., Masterman and Barlow, 17-18th c., with list of vicars, notes on monumental inscriptions, *etc.*

Adel
DRAPER, WILLIAM H. *Adel and its Norman church: a history of the parish and church, from the earliest down to the present time.* Leeds: Richard Jackson, 1906. Includes notes on the parish register, monumental inscriptions, and the clergy, *etc.*

Addingham
See Skipton

Adwalton
See Morley

Airedale
See Leeds

Allerton
See Manningham

Almondbury
HULBERT, CHARLES AUGUSTUS. *Annals of the church and parish of Almondbury, Yorkshire.* Longmans & Co., 1882. Contents: Pt. 1. The parish church of All Saints. Pt. 2. The halls, grammar school, and family history. Includes much information on families, monumental inscriptions, list of churchwardens, etc., etc.

Ardsley
See Morley

Bainton
OLLARD, S.L. 'Notes on the history of Bainton and its rectors', *Y.A.J.* **25**, 1908-9, 104-23. Medieval.

Barnsley
JACKSON, ROWLAND. *The history of the town and township of Barnsley in Yorkshire, from an early period.* Dell and Daldy, 1858. Includes folded pedigrees of Clarke, Chappel, Wood, Rooke, Usher, Becket, Armitage, Wentworth and Keresforth; also muster roll for the Wapentake of Staincross, 1589.

Barrowby
CUNIFFE, I.D., & ASHCROFT, M.Y. 'Barrowby in 1851: documents', *Journal* **4**. N.Y.C.R.O.P. **10**, 1976, 5-64. Includes tithe apportionment, census returns, directory extracts, *etc.*

Barwick in Elmet
COLMAN, F.S. *A history of the parish of Barwick-in-Elmet.* T.S. **17**. 1908. Includes numerous pedigrees, extracts from parochial and manorial records, various lists of tenants, *etc., etc.*

Batley

SHEARD, MICHAEL. *Records of the parish of Batley in the County of York: historical, topographical, ecclesiastical, testamentary and genealogical.* Worksop: Robert White, 1894. Includes many extracts from parish records, pedigrees, 81 wills, *etc.*
See also Morley

Bawtry

PECK, W. *A topographical history and description of Bawtry and Thorne, with the villages adjacent.* Doncaster: the author, 1813. Includes some monumental inscriptions.

Bedale

ASHCROFT, M.Y., ed. *Bedale 1772-1841.* N.Y.C.R.O.P. 3. 1975. Includes terrier c.1772, census return 1841, extract from tithe apportionment, 1839, *etc.*
MCCALL, HARRY BERTRAM. *The early history of Bedale in the North Riding of Yorkshire.* Elliot Stock, 1907. Descent; includes pedigrees of Stapleton, Fitz Alan, Grey, Deyncourt, Lovel, and Peirse.

Beverley

OLIVER, GEORGE. *The history and antiquities of the town and minster of Beverley, in the county of York, from the most early period, with historical and descriptive sketches of the abbeys of Watton and Meaux, the convent of Haltemprise, the villages of Cottingham, Leckonfield, Bishop and Cherry Burton, Walkington, Risby, Scorburgh, and the hamlets comprised within the liberties of Beverley ...* Beverley: M. Turner, 1829. Includes pedigrees of Hotham (folded), Heron, Stuteville, De Wake, Percy & Louvaine, Gee, Ellerker, Warton, Bethell, Machell and Bassett, *etc.*
POULSON, GEORGE. *Beverlac: or, the antiquities and history of the town of Beverley in the County of York, and of the provostry and collegiate establishment of St. John's, with a minute description of the present Minster and the church of St. Mary, and other ancient and modern edifices, compiled from authentic records, charters, and unpublished manuscripts.* 2 vols. Longman, Rees, Orme, Brown and Green, 1892. Extensive; includes folded pedigrees of Hotham, Gee, Legard and Warton.
FLOWER, CYRIL T. 'The Beverley town riots 1381-2', *Transactions of the Royal Historical Society* N.S., **19,** 1905, 79-99. Includes various lists of names.
See also the *Victoria County History* volume, cited under the East Riding in section 1 above.

Bingley

TURNER, J. HORSFALL. *Ancient Bingley, or, Bingley, its history and scenery.* Bingley: Thomas Harrison and Sons, 1897. Includes deed abstracts, extracts from court rolls, extracts from Quaker registers, tax lists, monumental inscriptions, pedigrees, *etc., etc.*

Birstall

CRADOCK, H.C. *A history of the ancient parish of Birstall, Yorkshire.* Society for Promoting Christian Knowledge, 1933. Includes much information on the clergy.
See also Morley

Bishop Burton
See Cherry Burton

Bishopthorpe

BRAYLEY, C.E.W. *The annals of Bishopthorpe 1215 to 1963.* York: H. Morley and Sons, 1964. Many names.

Bolton Abbey
See Skipton

Bradford

JAMES, DAVID. *Bradford.* Halifax: Ryburn Publishing, 1990. General history, 18-20th c.
JAMES, JOHN. *The history and topography of Bradford (in the County of York), with topographical notices of its parish.* 2 vols. Longman, Brown, Green & Longmans, 1841. Facsimile reprint, Queensbury: Mountain Press, 1967. Continued by his *Continuations & additions to the history of Bradford and its parish.* Longmans, Green, Reader & Dyer, 1866. Includes pedigrees and biographical notices.

CRUMP, W.B. 'The yeoman-clothier of the seventeenth century: his home and his loom-shop: a study of the inventories contained in the Bradford Local Record series, vol. 1', *B.A.* **7**, N.S., **5**, 1933, 217-39.

KODITSCHEK, THEODORE. *Class formation and urban-industrial society: Bradford, 1750-1850.* Cambridge: Cambridge University Press, 1990.

KODITSCHEK, THEODORE. 'The dynamics of class formation in nineteenth-century Bradford', in BEIER, A.L., CANNADINE, DAVID, & ROSENHEIM, JAMES M., eds. *The first modern society: essays in English history in honour of Lawrence Stone.* Cambridge: Cambridge University Press, 1989, 511-48.

REYNOLDS, JACK. *The great paternalist: Titus Salt and the growth of nineteenth-century Bradford.* Maurice Temple Smith, 1983.

WRIGHT, D.G., & JOWITT, J.A., eds. *Victorian Bradford: essays in honour of Jack Reynolds.* Bradford: City of Bradford Metropolitan Council Libraries Division, 1981.

ASHFORTH, DAVID. 'Settlement and removal in urban areas: Bradford, 1834-71', in ROSE, MICHAEL E., ed. *The poor and the city: the English poor law in its urban context, 1834-1914.* Leicester: Leicester University Press, 1985, 57-92. General discussion of the operation of the poor law.

PEACOCK, A.J. *Bradford chartism, 1838-1840.* Borthwick papers **36**. 1969.

ITTMANN, KARL. *Work, gender and family in Victorian England.* Macmillan, 1994. Study of Bradford.

ITTMANN, KARL. 'Family limitation and family economy in Bradford, West Yorkshire, 1851-1881', *Journal of social history* **25**(3), 1992, 547-73. Based on census data.

Brighouse

TURNER, J. HORSFALL. *The history of Brighouse, Rastrick and Hipperholme, with manorial notes on Coley, Lightcliffe, Northowram, Shelf, Fixby, Clifton and Kirklees.* Bingley: Thomas Harrison and Sons, 1893. Includes various lists of names, pedigrees, portraits, *etc.*

BARKE, MICHAEL. 'The population of Brighouse, West Yorkshire, in 1851', *Y.A.J.* **48**, 1976, 135-46. Based on census schedule.

Burley in Wharfedale

WARWICK, MARGARET, & WARWICK, DENNIS. 'Burley-in-Wharfedale in the nineteenth century: a study of social stratification and social mobility', *Local population studies* **54**, 1995, 40-55. Based on census returns, 1841-91.

Burstall Priory
See Holderness

Burstwick
'Spotlight on ... Burstwick', *B.T.* **53**, 1993, 21-5. Notes on, and extracts from, a variety of sources.

Calderdale
See Wharfedale

Calverley

KING, STEVE. 'Dying with style: infant death and its context in a rural industrial township, 1650-1830', *Social history of medicine* **10**(1), 1993, 3-24. Study based on Calverley cum Farsley parish registers.

KING, STEVEN. 'Migrants on the margin? Mobility, integration and occupation in the West Riding, 1650-1820', *Journal of historical geography* **23**(3), 1997, 284-304. Study of Calverley; includes chart shewing kinship connections of James Hargreaves (with Ask family, *etc.*).

KING, STEVE. 'Power, representation, and the historical individual: problems with sources for record linkage in two Yorkshire townships, 1650-1820', *Local historian* **27**(2), 1997, 78-90. Study of Calverley and Sowerby Bridge.

KING, STEVE. 'Record linkage in a protoindustrial community', *History and computing* **4**(1), 1992, 27-33. Based on parish registers of Sowerby and Calverley; includes extracts from the Calverley register relating to Ackroyd.

Carlinghow
See Morley

Churwell
See Morley

19

Claro Wapentake

SHEAHAN, JAMES JOSEPH. *History and topography of the Wapentake of Claro, being a supplementary volume to T. Whellan and Co's 'History of York and the North Riding'.* Beverley: John Green, 1871. Designated 'vol. III.' Parochial survey.

Cleckheaton

PEEL, FRANK. *Spen Valley, past and present.* Heckmondwicke: Senior and Co., 1893. Covers the parishes of Cleckheaton, Liversedge and Heckmondwike; includes chapter on the families of Liversedge, Rayner, and Neville, various lists of tenants, taxes, *etc.*

Cleveland

ATKINSON, J.C. *History of Cleveland, ancient and modern.* Barrow in Furness: J. Richardson, 1874. Includes a topographical survey of the parishes.

GRAVES, JOHN. *The history of Cleveland in the North Riding of the County of York, comprehending an historical and descriptive view of the ancient and present state of each parish within the Wapontake of Langbargh, the soil, produce and natural curiosities, with the origin and genealogy of the principal families within the district.* York: J. Todd, 1808. Reprinted Stockton on Tees: Patrick & Shatton, 1972. Parochial survey; includes folded pedigree of Chaloner of Guisborough and many other pedigrees.

ORD, JOHN WALKER. *The history and antiquities of Cleveland, comprising the Wapentake of East and West Langbargh, North Riding, County of York.* Simpkin and Marshall, 1846. Reprinted Durham: J. Shatton, 1980. Parochial survey, with various pedigrees.

Clifton
See Brighouse

Coley
See Brighouse

Conisbrough
See Doncaster

Copgrove

MAJOR, HENRY D.A. *Memorials of Copgrove, together with the parish registers from A.D. 1584 to 1790.* Oxford: Basil Blackwell, 1922. Parochial history; includes will of John Brown 1805, list of rectors and patrons, *etc.*

Cottingham
See Beverley

Cottingley

PRESTON, W.E. 'Cottingley: its early history', *B.A.* 7; N.S., 5, 1933, 77-97. Includes folded pedigree of Franke of Alwoodley and Cottingley, 16-17th c.
See also Morley.

Craven

WHITAKER, THOMAS DUNHAM. *The history and antiquities of the Deanery of Craven,* ed. Alfred W. Morant. 3rd ed. Leeds: Joseph Dodgson, 1878. Extensive parochial survey; many folded pedigrees.

MID-WHARFEDALE LOCAL HISTORY RESEARCH GROUP. 'Parish Register Occupation Project: a comparison between the Craven muster roll and parish registers', *Local population studies* **40**, 1988, 61-3.

Crayke

HEYWORTH, P.L. 'Crayke: a seventeenth century peculiar', *Y.A.J.* **40**, 1962, 662-4. Includes list of 'those which keep greyhounds', late 17th c.

Cross Stone

NEWELL, ABRAHAM. 'Cross Stone', *P.R.H.A.S.* 1928, 161-222. Includes 'rental', i.e., rate assessment, 1751, *etc.*

Dewsbury

GREENWOOD, JOHN BESWICKE. *The early ecclesiastical history of Dewsbury, in the West Riding of the County of York, including a sketch of the introduction of Christianity into Northumbria to which are added, with notes, Dr. Whitaker's account of Dewsbury from his 'Loidis and Elmete', and his dissertation on the origin and progress of domestic architecture from his 'History of Whalley', and an account of the Savile family of Lupset, Thornhill and Howley.* John Russell Smith, 1859. Includes notes from the parish register.

Doncaster

MILLER, EDWARD. *The history and antiquities of Doncaster and its vicinity, with anecdotes of eminent men.* Doncaster: W. Sheardown, 1804. Includes 'memoirs of eminent men', and a parochial survey of towns and villages situated within 6 to 10 miles of Doncaster.

TOMLINSON, JOHN. *Doncaster, from the Roman occupation to the present time.* Doncaster: John Tomlinson, 1887. Extensive antiquarian study.

WAINWRIGHT, JOHN. *Yorkshire: an historical and topographical introduction to a knowledge of the ancient state of the Wapentake of Strafford and Tickhill, with ample accounts of Doncaster and Conisbrough, and of the villages, hamlets, churches, antiquities and other matters connected therewith.* Sheffield: John Blackwell, 1829. v.1. only published, contains accounts of Doncaster and Conisburgh, and an extensive introduction, with pedigrees and biographical notices, *etc.*

Doncaster Deanery

HUNTER, JOSEPH. *South Yorkshire: the history and topography of the Deanery of Doncaster in the Diocese and County of York.* 2 vols. J.B. Nichols and Son, 1828-31. Reprinted in facsimile, with introduction by George R. Potter. East Ardsley: E.P. Publishing, 1974. Parochial survey, with descents of manors, lists of clergy, many pedigrees, *etc.*

Driffield

ROSS, FRED K. *Contributions towards a history of Driffield and the surrounding Wolds district in the East Riding of the County of York.* Driffield: Thomas Holderness, 1898. Includes many biographical notes, lists of clergy (Anglican and non-conformist), list of landowners from the 'new Domesday' book of 1874, *etc.*

Easingwold

GILL, THOMAS. *Vallis Eboracensis, comprising the history and antiquities of Easingwold and its neighbourhood.* Simpkin, Marshall and Co., 1852. Includes notes on families, monumental inscriptions, *etc.*

MALTBY, BESSIE. 'Easingwold marriage horizons', *Local population studies* **2**, 1969, 36-9. Based on parish registers.

Ecclesall

PAULUS, CAROLUS. *Unpublished pages relating to the manor and parish of Ecclesall, including the enclosure of the common and waste lands there.* Sheffield: J.W. Northend, 1927. Includes enclosure award, 1788, and rates assessment 1786.

Ecclesfield

EASTWOOD, JONATHAN. *History of the parish of Ecclesfield in the County of York.* Bell & Daldy, 1862. Includes notes on the descents of properties, *etc.*

HEY, DAVID. *The village of Ecclesfield.* Huddersfield: Advertiser Press, 1968. Includes list of inhabitants from *White's directory*, 1833.

Farsley
See Calverley

Fixby
See Brighouse

Fountains Abbey
See Ripon

Fylingdales

STORM, ALAN. 'Seasonality of births and marriages in a seafaring community before the age of steam', *Local population studies* **52**, 1994, 43-7. Based on the parish registers of Fylingdales, particularly relating to Robin Hood's Bay.

Giggleswick

BRAYSHAW, THOMAS, & ROBINSON, RALPH M. *A history of the ancient parish of Giggleswick, which included the townships of Giggleswick, Settle, Rathmell, Langcliffe and Stainforth.* Halton & Co., 1932.

Gildersome

BOOTH, PHILIP HENRY. *History of Gildersome and the Booth family.* [ ], 1920. *See also* Morley

Gilling West Wapentake

PLANTAGENET-HARRISON, G.H.DE S.N. *The history of Yorkshire: Wapentake of Gilling West.* Hazell Watson and Viney, 1879. Extensive parochial survey, with many pedigrees – but be cautious!

Goodmanham

'Spotlight on ... Goodmanham', *B.T.* **54,** 1993, 20-24. Notes on, and extracts from, a variety of sources.

Guiseley

SLATER, PHILEMON. *History of the ancient parish of Guiseley, with introductory chapters on the antiquities of the district.* Hamilton Adams & Co., 1880. Many names.

Hackfall

See Ripon

Halifax

CRABTREE, JOHN. *A concise history of the parish and vicarage of Halifax, in the County of York.* Halifax: Hartley and Walker, 1836. Includes some monumental inscriptions.

WATSON, JOHN. *The history and antiquities of the parish of Halifax in Yorkshire.* T. Lowndes, 1775. Reprinted Didsbury: E.J. Morten, 1973. Includes much information on property descents.

SMAIL, JOHN. *The origins of middle-class culture: Halifax, Yorkshire, 1660-1780.* Ithaca: Cornell University Press, 1994. Scholarly.

SMAIL, JOHN. 'Manufacturer or artisan? The relationship between economic and cultural change in the early stages of the eighteenth-century industrialization', *Journal of social history* **25**(4), 1992, 791-814. Based on Halifax probate inventories.

Haltemprise

See Beverley

Harewood

JONES, JOHN. *The history and antiquities of Harewood, in the county of York, with topographical notices of its parish and neighbourhood.* Simpkin Marshall and Co., 1859. Includes much genealogical information.

Harrogate

GRAINGE, WILLIAM. *The history and topography of Harrogate and the Forest of Knaresborough.* John Russell Smith, 1871. Parochial survey; including notes on families.

JENNINGS, BERNARD, ed. *A history of Harrogate & Knaresborough.* Huddersfield: Advertiser Press, 1970.

Harthill

GARBETT, HARRY. *The history of Harthill-w-Woodall and its hamlet Kiveton Park (the latter until 1868 when it became part of Wales parish).* Ilfracombe: Arthur H. Stockwell, 1950. Addenda includes 'lords of the manors of Harthill', 'list of known rectors', 'Leeds family, chief lords of manor of Harthill A.D. 1674 to present (1947)', 'minor scholarship winners Harthill Council School, 1897-1949', 'roll of honour ... 1939-1945', list of 'old families still resident in Harthill', *etc.*

Headley

PRETTON, W. 'Headley in Bradford-Dale', *B.A.* **8**; N.S. **6**, 1940, 91-116. Includes folded pedigree of Midgley of Thornton and Clayton, 17-18th c.

Heaton

See Manningham

Heckmondwike

See Cleckheaton

Hedon

BOYLE, JOHN R. *The early history of the town and port of Hedon, in the East Riding of the County of York.* Hull: A. Brown & Sons, 1895. Includes charters, churchwardens' accounts, bailiffs' accounts, and other extracts from original sources.

CRAVEN, MARTIN T. *A new and complete history of the Borough of Hedon.* Driffield: Ridings Publishing Co., 1972. Includes pedigree of Iveson, 16-19th c., various lists of names, *etc.*

Helmsley

MCDONNELL, J., ed. *A history of Helmsley, Rievaulx and district.* York: Stonegate Press, 1963. Includes pedigrees of Crosland and Sandwith, list of vicars of Helmsley, list of Catholic recusants, *etc.*

Hemingbrough

BURTON, THOMAS. *The history and antiquities of the parish of Hemingbrough in the county of York,* ed. James Raine. Y.A.S. extra series [1.] 1888. Includes inscriptions, list of clergy, parish register extracts, various pedigrees, *etc., etc.*

Hessay

NEWMAN, P.R. 'The Hessay enclosure of 1831: a study in the economic and social history of an Ainsty township in the 19th century', *Journal* **9**; N.Y.C.R.O.P. **29**, 1982, 89-165. Includes census returns, 1841-71.

Hipperholme
See Brighouse

Holderness

POULSON, GEORGE. *The history and antiquities of the seigniory of Holderness, in the East Riding of the county of York, including the abbeys of Meaux and Swine, with the priories of Nunkeeling and Burstall, compiled from authentic charters, records and the unpublished manuscripts of the Rev. William Dade, remaining in the library of Burton Constable.* 2 vols. Hull: Robert Brown, 1840. Parochial survey, including lists of clergy, monumental inscriptions, many pedigrees, manorial descents, *etc.*

ENGLISH, BARBARA. *The lords of Holderness: 1086-1260: a study in feudal society.* Oxford: Oxford University Press, 1979. *See also* Withernsea

Howdenshire

SALTMARSHE, P. 'Some Howdenshire villages', *T.E.R.A.S.* **13**(2), 1907, 153-88. Includes pedigrees of Sothill and Hotham, notes on the descent of farms, *etc.*

Howley Hall
See Morley

Huddersfield

HAIGH, E.A. HILARY, ed. *Huddersfield: a most handsome town. Aspects of the history and culture of a West Yorkshire town.* Huddersfield: Kirklees Cultural Services, 1992. Scholarly collection of essays.

SYKES, D.F.E. *The history of Huddersfield and its vicinity.* Huddersfield: Advertiser Press, 1898. Includes notes on many families.

SYKES, D.F.E. *The history of Huddersfield and the valleys of the Colne, the Holme and the Dearne.* Huddersfield: The Worker Press, [190-?] With various lists of names, including lists of voters in 1807.

BROOKE, ALAN, & KIPLING, LESLEY. *Liberty or death: radicals, republicans or Luddites, 1793-1823.* Horley: Workers History, 1993. Study of the Huddersfield area.

Hull

The authoritative history of Hull is in the *Victoria County History* volume cited above under the East Riding in section 1.

CALVERT, HUGH. *A history of Kingston upon Hull, from the earliest times to the present day.* Chichester: Phillimore & Co., 1978. Modern study.

FROST, CHARLES. *Notices relative to the early history of the town and port of Hull, compiled from original records and unpublished manuscripts and illustrated with engravings, etchings and vignettes.* J.B. Nichols, 1827. Includes pedigrees of De La Pole and Sutton, and many extracts from original sources.

GENT, THOMAS. *Gent's history of Hull (Annales regioduni Hullini), in fac-simile of the original of 1735, to which is appended notices of the life and works of Thomas Gent, printer, of York.* Hull: M.C. Peck and Son, 1869. Originally published Ward & Chandler, *et al,* 1735. Includes inscriptions, list of mayors and sheriffs, *etc.*

GILLETT, EDWARD, & MACMAHON, KENNETH A. *A history of Hull.* Oxford: Oxford University Press, 1980.

HADLEY, GEORGE. *A new and complete history of the town and county of the town of Kingston-upon-Hull ...* Hull: T. Briggs, 1788. Not seen.

TICKELL, JOHN. *The history of the town and county of Kingston upon Hull, from its foundations in the reign of Edward the First to the present time, with a description of part of the adjacent country.* Hull: Thomas Lee and Co., 1798. Extensive; includes lists of mayors and sheriffs, *etc.*

HEATH, PETER. 'Urban piety in the later middle ages: the evidence of Hull wills', in DOBSON, BARRIE, ed. *The church, politics and patronage in the fifteenth century.* Gloucester: Alan Sutton, 1984. 209-34.

CROSS, CLAIRE. 'Northern women in the early modern period: the female testators of Hull and Leeds, 1520-1650', *Y.A.J.* **59**, 1987, 83-94. General discussion.

JACKSON, GORDON. *Hull in the eighteenth century: a study in economic and social history.* Oxford University Press for the University of Hull, 1972.

JACKSON, GORDON. *The trade and shipping of eighteenth-century Hull.* E.Y.L.H.S. **31**. 1975.

BELLAMY, JOYCE M. *The trade and shipping of nineteenth-century Hull.* E.Y.L.H.S. **27**. 1971.

See also Leeds

Ilkley
COLLYER, ROBERT, & TURNER, J. HORSFALL. *Ilkley: ancient and modern.* Otley: Wm. Walker & Sons, 1885. Includes many deeds, notes on parish records, pedigrees, *etc.*

Ingleby Arncliffe
'Ingleby Arncliffe', *Y.A.J.* **16**, 1900-1901, 121-226. Includes deeds, pew list of 1604/5, monumental inscriptions, list of clergy, descent of the manor, pedigree of Mauleverer, medieval-18th c., rental of Arncliffe, 1434, wills, etc.

Keighley
GARRETT, EILIDH M. 'The trials of labour: motherhood versus employment in a nineteenth-century textile centre', *Continuity and change* **5**, 1990, 121-54. Based on census returns for Keighley, 1851-81.

Keyingham
SMITH, M.H. *Parish registers and population in South Holderness: some researches into the parish registers of Keyingham, Patrington and Winestead.* Hedon local history series 3. Hedon: Hedon and District Local History Society, 1976. Demographic study.

Kirby Moorside
EASTMEAD, W. *Historia Rievallensis, containing the history of Kirby Moorside, and an account of the most important places in its vicinity, together with brief notices of the more remote or less important ones ...* Baldwin, Cradock and Joy, 1824.

Kirby Underdale
SHEPHERD, W.R. *The history of Kirby Underdale.* Batley: J.S. Newsome & Son, 1928. See also supplement, 1930, and appendices, 1932 and 1939. Includes chapters on the registers, the rectors, the Bourchiers, the Remingtons, *etc., etc.*

WALGATE, RICHARD E. 'Kirby Underdale', *B.T.* **15**, 1983, 7-9. Includes names from inscriptions, hearth tax return 1672, poor assessment, 1685, etc.

Kirkburton
MOREHOUSE, HENRY JAMES. *The history and topography of the parish of Kirkburton and of the graveship of Holme, including Holmfirth, in the County of York.* Huddersfield: H. Roebuck, 1861. Includes monumental inscriptions, pedigrees, and many other names.

Kirkby Malham
MORKILL, JOHN WILLIAM. *The parish of Kirby Malhamdale, in the West Riding of Yorkshire.* Gloucester: John Bellows, 1933. Includes deeds, pedigrees, biographical notices, notes on parochial records, *etc., etc.*

Kirkby Overblow
SPEIGHT, HARRY. *Kirkby Overblow and district, being a record of the history, antiquities, folk-lore, and old customs of the ancient parish of Kirkby Overblow in the West Riding of Yorkshire, with brief notices of adjacent places.* Elliot Stock, 1903. Includes much information on families, as well as a list of subscribers.

Kirklees
See Brighouse

Kiveton Park
See Harthill

Knaresborough

CALVERT, M. *The history of Knaresbrough, comprising an accurate and detailed account of the Castle, the Forest, and the several townships included in the said parish.* Knaresborough: W. Parr, 1844. Includes monumental inscriptions, *etc.*

Knaresborough Forest
See Harrogate

Langbaurgh Wapentake
See Cleveland

Langcliffe
See Giggleswick

Leckonfield
See Beverley

Leeds

FRASER, DEREK, ed. *A history of modern Leeds.* Manchester: Manchester University Press, 1980. Collection of essays, 18-20th c.

THORESBY, RALPH. *Ducatus Leodiensis, or, the topography of the ancient and populous town and parish of Leedes and parts adjacent, in the West Riding of the County of York, &c., &c.* 2nd ed., edited by Thomas Dunham Whitaker. Leeds: Robinson Son and Holdsworth, 1816. Includes many pedigrees, some folded.

WARDELL, JAMES. *The municipal history of the Borough of Leeds in the County of York from the earliest period to the election of the first mayor under the provisions of the Municipal Corporation Act 1836, including numerous extracts from the court books of the Corporation [1662-1807], and an appendix containing copies and translations of charters and other documents relating to the borough.* Longman Brown & Co., 1846.

WHITAKER, T.D. *Loidis and Elmete, or, an attempt to illustrate the districts described in those words by Bede, and supposed to embrace the lower portions of Aredale and Wharfdale, together with the entire Vale of Calder, in the County of York.* Leeds: Robinson Son and Holdsworth, 1816. Extensive; includes many pedigrees and monumental inscriptions, *etc.,* with notes on many local parishes in what was the ancient British kingdom of Elmet.

LUMB, G.D. 'A Thoresby manuscript', in *Miscellanea* 1; *T.S.* 2, 1891, 152-77. Maimed soldiers' accounts, 1676-9; also brief extracts from Leeds parish register, 1550-64, and monumental inscriptions from St. Peters, Leeds, *etc.*

RUSBY, JAMES. 'Miscellaneous genealogical notes', *Miscellanea* 1. *T.S.* 2. 1891, 36-50. Relating to Leeds.

LONSDALE, ALLISTER. 'A note on Leeds wills, 1539-1561', in *The Thoresby miscellany* 14. T.S. 50. 1968, 78-85. Study of religious changes revealed in wills.

CROSS, C. 'Wills as evidence of popular piety in the Reformation period: Leeds and Hull, 1540-1640', in LOADES, D.M., ed. *The end of strife: papers selected from the proceedings of the Commission Internationale d'Histoire Ecclésiastique Comparée held at the University of Durham, 2 to 9 September 1981.* Edinburgh: T. & T. Clark, 1984, 44-51. General discussion of their use as evidence.

BERESFORD, MAURICE. *East End, West End: the face of Leeds during urbanisation 1684-1842.* T.S. 60-61. 1988. Scholarly; includes good bibliography and various lists of names.

'Building history from fire insurance records: an autobiographical fragment', in BERESFORD, M.W. *Time and place: collected essays.* Hambledon Press, 1985, 263-74. Originally published *Urban history yearbook* 1976, 7-14. Methodological essay, largely concerned with Leeds.

BERESFORD, M.W. 'Prometheus insured: the Sun Fire Agency in Leeds during urbanization, 1716-1826', *Economic history review* 35(3), 1982, 373-89. Includes list of policies for over £10,000.

BARNARD, SYLVIA M. *To prove I'm not forgot: living and dying in a Victorian city.* Manchester: Manchester University Press, 1990. A study of death in Leeds.

MORGAN, JIM. 'The burial question in Leeds in the eighteenth and nineteenth centuries', in HOULBROOKE, RALPH, ed. *Death, ritual and bereavement.* Routledge, 1989, 95-104. Study of burial practices.

MORRIS, R.J. *Class, sect and party: the making of the British middle class. Leeds, 1820-1850.* Manchester: Manchester University Press, 1990.

WARD, DAVID. 'Environs and neighbours in the 'two nations': residential differentiation in mid nineteenth-century Leeds', *Journal of historical geography* **6**, 1980, 133-62.

TREEN, C. 'The process of suburban development in north Leeds, 1870-1914', in THOMPSON, F.M.L., ed. *The rise of suburbia.* [Leicester]: Leicester University Press, 1982, 158-209.

See also Hull

Lightcliffe
See Brighouse

Liversedge
See Cleckheaton

Malton
HUDLESTON, N.A. *History of Malton and Norton.* Scarborough: G.A. Pindar & Son, 1962. Many names.

SALMON, D.J., ed. *Malton in the early nineteenth century.* N.Y.C.R.O.P. **26**. 1981. Includes survey of Earl Fitzwilliam's property in the 1840s, listing occupiers.

Manningham
CUDWORTH, WILLIAM. *Manningham, Heaton and Allerton (townships of Bradford), treated historically and topographically.* Bradford: W. Cudworth, 1896. Many extracts from original sources.

Masham/Mashamshire
FISHER, JOHN. *The history and antiquities of Masham and Mashamshire, together with an account of its several franchises, its ancient lords, rectors, prebendaries, vicars, curates, &c., &c., and appendices containing copies of several charters, grants and other important documents relating to the manor, forest, freewarren and free chase, markets, fairs, prebendal church, &c., of Masham.* Simpkin Marshall and Co., 1865.

Meaux Abbey
See Beverley and Holderness

Meltham
HUGHES, JOSEPH. *The history of the township of Meltham, near Huddersfield, in the West Riding of the County of York, from the earliest times to the present.* John Russell Smith, 1866. Includes extracts from the parish register, monumental inscriptions, manorial descent, *etc.*

Metham
SALTMARSHE, P. 'Some Howdenshire villages', *T.E.R.A.S.* **15**, 1908, 71-84; **16**, 1909, 1-49. Study of Metham including extensive notes on descent of the Metham family, including pedigrees, 14-20th c.

Methley
DARBYSHIRE, HUBERT STANLEY, & LUMB, GEORGE DENISON, eds. *The history of Methley.* T.S. **35**. 1937. Includes list of rectors, extracts from manorial rolls, notes on the parish register, list of persons liable to be rated 1592, deed extracts, *etc.*

YASUMOTO, MINORU. 'Industrialisation and demographic change in a Yorkshire parish', *Local population studies* **27**, 1981, 10-25. Based on the parish registers of Methley, 17-19th c.

Middlesbrough
MOORSOM, NORMAN. 'Sources of Middlesbrough's history', *C.T.L.H.S.B.* **1**, 1968, unpaginated. Brief note.

Middleton
See Morley

Moor Monkton
NEWMAN, P.R. *Moor Monkton and its people 1600 to 1916: aspects of the social and economic history of a township in the Ainsty of York.* York: [ ], 1982. Modern study.

Morley
SCATCHERD, NORRISON. *The history of Morley, in the parish of Batley and West Riding of Yorkshire, and especially of the old chapel in that village, with some account of Ardsley, Topcliffe, Woodchurch, Batley, Howley-Hall, Soothill Hall, Carlinghow, Birstall, Usher-Hall, Adwalton, the battle of Adwalton Moor, the battle of Dunbar, Gildersome, Churwell, Cottingley, Middleton, Thorpe, and other places in the vicinity, also, of remarkable occurrences in these parts in the seventeenth century.* Leeds: J. Heaton, 1830.

SMITH, WILLIAM. *The history and antiquities of Morley, in the West Riding.* Longmans Green & Co., 1876. Includes descent of the manor, and 'biographical sketches' of prominent personalities.

SMITH, WILLIAM. *Morley: ancient and modern.* Longmans Green and Co., 1886. Many names.

Nafferton

'Nafferton', *B.T.* **20**, 1984, 17-21. Includes extracts from Baines' *directory,* 1823, land tax 1783, list of poor, 1823, 1851 census, rate list 1743, *etc.*

'Spotlight on ... Nafferton', *B.T.* **56**, 1993, 22-7. Notes on, and extracts from, a variety of sources, including Bulmer's 1892 *Directory.*

Netherthong

MOREHOUSE, H.J., & BROOKE, THOMAS. 'The township of Nether-Thong', *Y.A.J.* **13**, 1895, 193-212. Includes notes on the families of Wilson (including pedigree, 16-18th c.), Woodhead, Kaye, Berry, and Newton.

Newton Kyme

BRUCE, WILLIAM D. 'An account of the parish of Newton Kyme, in the County of York', *Topographer & genealogist* **1**, 1846, 500-5. Brief; includes descent of the manor, monumental inscriptions, and list of rectors.

Nidderdale

JENNINGS, BERNARD, ed. *A history of Nidderdale.* 2nd ed. Pateley Bridge: Nidderdale History Group, 1983.

SPEIGHT, HARRY. *Nidderdale from Nun Monkton to Whernside, being a record of the history, antiquities, scenery, old homes, families, &c., of the beautiful valley of the Nidd.* Elliot Stock, 1906. Includes many pedigrees; appendices include INMAN, ALFRED H. 'A short account of the family of Inman of Nidderdale.'

SUMMERBRIDGE TUTORIAL GROUP. *Kith and kin: Nidderdale families 1500-1750,* ed. Maurice Turner. [Summerbridge]: The Group, 1995. Scholarly study based on parish registers, probate records, tax returns, *etc.*

Northallerton

INGLEDEW, C.J. DAVISON. *The history and antiquities of Northallerton, in the County of York.* Bell and Daldy, 1858. Includes pedigrees of Lascelles, also Metcalfe and Markwood, various wills, extensive extracts from parish registers, list of vicars, *etc.*

SAYWELL, J.L. *The history and annals of Northallerton, Yorkshire, with notes and voluminous appendix, compiled from authentic and reliable sources.* Northallerton: J. Vasey, 1885. Many names — but unfortunately no index.

Northowram

See Brighouse

Norton

'Spotlight on ... Norton', *B.T.* **55**, 1993, 23-30. See also **56**, 1993, 27. Extracts from, and notes on, a variety of sources, including a full copy of the entry in Bulmer's 1892 *directory.*

Nunburnholme

MORRIS, M.C.F. *Nunburnholme: its history and antiquities.* Henry Frowde, 1907. Includes chapters on 'The rectors', 'Parish registers', and 'families', and includes will of William Braithwaite 1601, with various deed abstracts.

Nunkeeling Priory

See Holderness

Patrington

See Keyingham

Penistone

DRANSFIELD, JOHN N. *A history of the parish of Penistone.* Penistone: James H. Wood, 1906. Extensive; includes pedigrees.

STARK, MARGARET. 'History of Penistone', *F.S.* **8**(2), 1987, 46-8; **8**(3), 1988, 65-8; **8**(4), 1988, 97-8; **9**(1), 1988, 11-12; **9**(2), 1988, 49-50. Extracts from various sources; many names.

Pocklington

BELLINGHAM, ROGER A. 'The use of marriage horizons to measure migration: some conclusions from a study of Pocklington, East Yorkshire, in the late eighteenth century', *Local population studies* **44**, 1990, 52-5. Based on parish registers.

Pontefract

BOOTHROYD, B. *The history of the ancient borough of Pontefract, containing an interesting account of its castle, and the three different sieges it sustained during the Civil War, with notes and pedigrees of some of the most distinguished royalists and Parliamentarians, chiefly drawn from manuscripts never before published.* Pontefract: the author, 1807.

FOX, GEORGE. *The history of Pontefract in Yorkshire.* Pontefract: John Fox, 1827. Includes various lists of names.

Pudsey

RAYNER, SIMEON. *The history & antiquities of Pudsey.* ed. William Smith. Longmans Green and Co., 1887. Includes biographical sketches, monumental inscriptions, deed abstracts, lists of parish officers, *etc.*

Rastrick

See Brighouse

Rathmell

See Giggleswick

Richmond

CLARKSON, CHRISTOPHER. *The history of Richmond in the County of York.* Richmond: the author, 1821. Includes folded pedigrees of Wharton, Stapleton, Yorke and Scrope.

FIELDHOUSE, R., & JENNINGS, B. *A history of Richmond and Swaledale.* Chichester: Phillimore & Co., 1978. Scholarly study.

Richmondshire

FIELDHOUSE, R. 'Social structure from Tudor lay subsidies and probate inventories: a case study: Richmondshire (Yorkshire)', *Local population studies* **12**, 1974, 9-24.

POLLARD, A.J. 'The Richmondshire community of gentry during the Wars of the Roses', in ROSS, CHARLES, ed. *Patronage, pedigree, and power in later medieval England.* Gloucester: Alan Sutton, 1979, 37-59. Includes pedigree of Conyers of Hornby.

WHITAKER, THOMAS DUNHAM. *A history of Richmondshire, in the North Riding of the County of York, together with three parts of the Everwickshire of Domesday which form the Wapentakes of Lonsdale, Ewecross, and Amunderness, in the counties of York, Lancaster and Westmoreland.* 2 vols. Longman, Hurst, Rees, Orme and Brown, 1823. Includes many pedigrees, some folded.

Rievaulx

See Helmsley and Kirby Moorside

Ripon

FARRER, WILLIAM. *The history of Ripon, comprehending a civil and ecclesiastical account of that ancient borough, to which is added a description of Fountains Abbey, Studley, and Hackfall, and an appendix, containing charters, &c., illustrative of the work.* Ripon: W. Farrer, 1801. Includes monumental inscriptions.

GENT, THOMAS. *The antient and modern history of the loyal town of Rippon ...* York: Printing-Office, 1733. Includes lists of the 'wakemen' and mayors, monumental inscriptions, *etc.*

HARRISON, WILLIAM. *Ripon millenary: a record of the festival, also a history of the city, arranged under its wakemen and mayors from the year 1400.* Ripon: W. Harrison, 1892. With biographical notes on wakemen and mayors, *etc.*

Risby

See Beverley

Robin Hoods Bay

See Fylingdales

Rotherham

GUEST, JOHN. *Yorkshire. Historic notices of Rotherham, eccesiastical, collegiate and civil.* Worksop: Robert White, 1879. Extensive; includes parish register, 1542-1668, monumental inscriptions, numerous extracts from original sources, *etc., etc.*

'The Jordans, Jordan Dam', *R. & D.F.H.S.N.* **1**, 1984, 3-6. At Rotherham; includes many extracts from the parish register, 1765-1829.

Ryecroft

ROBERTSHAW, WILFRID. 'The settlement of Ryecroft in Tong', *B.A.* **8**; N.S., **6**, 1940, 141-59. Includes folded pedigrees of Nettleton, 17-18th c. and Balme, 18-20th c., also probate inventory of Judith Nettleton, 1707.

Saddleworth

WILD, M.T. 'The Saddleworth parish registers as a source for the history of the West Riding textiles industry during the eighteenth century', *Textile history* 1(2), 1969, 214-32.

Saltmarshe

SALTMARSHE, PHILIP. *History of the township and family of Saltmarshe in the East Riding of Yorkshire.* York: Ben Johnson and Company, 1910. Includes various lists of names and much information on the Saltmarshe family, with folded pedigree, 12-19th c.

Scarborough

BAKER, JOSEPH BROGDEN. *The history of Scarborough from the earliest date.* Longmans Green & Co., 1882. Extensive; includes a chapter of biographies.

HINDERWELL, THOMAS. *The history and antiquities of Scarborough.* 3rd ed. revised. Scarborough: M. Bye, 1832. Includes lists of names of subscribers for the building of Christ Church, Scarborough, 1828.

BINNS, JACK. *A place of great importance: Scarborough in the Civil Wars, 1640-1660.* Preston: Carnegie Publishing, 1996. Scholarly.

Scorborough

See Beverley

Selby

MORRELL, WILBERFORCE. *The history and antiquities of Selby in the West Riding of the County of York, containing its ancient and present state, ecclesiastical and civil, collected from various public records and other authentic evidences, with notices of the neighbouring parish of Brayton, and the townships of Thorpe*

Willoughby, Burn, Barlow, Hambleton and Gateforth. Selby: W.B. Bellerby, 1867. Includes many extracts from original sources.

MOUNTAIN, JAMES. *The history of Selby, ancient and modern, containing the most remarkable transactions, ecclesiastical, civil and military, from the earliest accounts to the present period, interspersed with portions of general history connected with the subject.* York: Edward Peck for the author, 1800. Includes directory of Selby.

Settle

See Giggleswick

Sheffield

DRURY, CHARLES. *A sheaf of essays by a Sheffield antiquary.* Sheffield: J.W. Northend, 1929. Essays on Sheffield history.

HALL, T.WALTER. *Incunabula of Sheffield history.* Sheffield: J.W.Northend, 1937. Collection of essays on Sheffield, including one on 'The Fairbanks of Sheffield'.

HUNTER, JOSEPH. *Hallamshire: the history and topography of the parish of Sheffield, in the county of York, with historical and descriptive notices of the parishes of Ecclesfield, Hansworth, Treeton, and Whiston, and of the chapelry of Bradfield.* New ed. by Alfred Gatty. Virtue and Co., 1869. Extensive; includes many pedigrees and extracts from original sources.

LINTON, DAVID L., ed. *Sheffield and its region: a scientific and historical survey.* Sheffield: British Association, 1956. Collection of authoritative essays.

BUCKATZSH, E.J. 'Occupations in the parish registers of Sheffield, 1655-1719', *Economic history review* 2nd series **1**, 1949, 145-50. Based on parish registers.

LEADER, ROBERT EADON. *Sheffield in the eighteenth century.* 2nd ed. Sheffield: Sir W.C. Leng & Co., 1905. General history.

TWEEDALE, GEOFFREY. *Steel city: entrepeneurship strategy and technology in Sheffield, 1743-1993.* Oxford: Clarendon Press, 1995. Modern urban history, with useful bibliography.

BINFIELD, CLYDE, et al, eds. *The history of the city of Sheffield, 1843-1993.* 3 vols. Sheffield: Sheffield Academic, 1993, v.1. Politics. v.2. Society. v.3. Images. Extensive; includes useful bibliography.

HARRISON, SAMUEL. *A complete history of the great flood at Sheffield on March 11th and 12th, 1864 ...* S. Harrison, 1864. Includes 'list of the dead and missing', which is also reprinted in:

PERKINS, JOHN. 'A list of the dead and missing in the Sheffield flood', *F.S.* 11(2), 1990, 44-8.

WARDALE, RICHARD. 'The aftermath of the Sheffield flood, 1864', *F.S.* 7, 1986-7, 49-50, 70-71 & 101-3. Lists damages claimed by those who suffered loss.

STAINTON, J.H. *The making of Sheffield, 1865-1914.* Sheffield: E. Weston & Sons, 1924. Includes numerous 'Sheffield's life stories'.

WILLIAMS, NAOMI. 'Death in its season: class, environment and the mortality of infants in nineteenth century Sheffield', *Social history of medicine* 5(1), 1992, 71-94. Based on civil and parish registers, and on 1871 census returns.

SMITH, DENNIS. *Conflict and compromise: class formation in English society. A comparative study of Birmingham and Sheffield.* Routledge & Kegan Paul, 1982. Scholarly study of the 19th c., with useful bibliography.

Shelf
See Brighouse

Skipton
DAWSON, W. HARBUTT. *History of Skipton (W.R. Yorks).* Skipton: Edmondson & Co., 1882. Reprinted Manchester: E.J. Morten, 1972. Includes various lists of names, e.g. lay subsidy 1379, monumental inscriptions, biographical notes on clergy, 'worthies', and headmasters of the grammar school, *etc.*

LONG, MOIRA, & MALTBY, BESSIE. 'Personal mobility in three West Riding parishes 1777-1812', *Local population studies* 24, 1980, 13-25. Based on the registers of Skipton, Bolton Abbey, and Addingham.

Snaith
ROBINSON, C.B. *History of the Priory and peculiar of Snaith in the County of York.* Simpkin Marshall and Co., 1861. Parish history; primarily biographical in character.

Snape
See Well

Soothill Hall
See Morley

South Cave
HALL, JOHN GEORGE. *A history of South Cave and of other parishes in the East Riding of the County of York.* Hull: Edwin Ombler, 1892. Includes several pedigrees.

South Holderness
See Withernsea

Sowerby Bridge
BAYLISS, D.G., & BAYLISS, H.E. 'Sowerby Bridge in 1851: some census details', *T. Hal.A.S.* 1984, 1-15. Sociological analysis; *not* a transcript.
See also Calverley

Staincliffe
See Giggleswick

Studley
See Ripon

Swaledale
See Wensleydale

Swine
THOMPSON, THOMAS. *A history of the church and priory of Swine, in Holderness.* John Nichols & Son, 1824.
See also Holderness

Thirsk
'A personal census: the final round: presentation to Mr. Richard Prest', *J.Cl.F.H.S.* 5(5), 1993, 17-19. Lists signatories to a testimonial to a postman's service in Thirsk, 1904.

Thorne
See Bawtry

Thorpe
See Morley

Tong Street
REDMONDS, GEORGE. 'Tong Street', *O.W.R.*
1(2), 1981, 31-4. Notes on families in the
'street', *etc.*

Topcliffe
,See Morley

Usher Hall
See Morley

Wakefield
WALKER, J.W. *Wakefield: its history and
people.* Wakefield: West Yorkshire
Printing Co., 1934. Extensive.
WATERS, S.H. *Wakefield in the seventeenth
century: a social history of the town
and neighbourhood from 1550-1710.*
Wakefield: Sanderson & Clayton,
1933.

Walkington
See Beverley

Wath upon Dearne
MARTIN, W. KEBLE. *A history of the
ancient parish of Wath-upon-Dearne
(South Yorks).* Wath upon Dearne: W.E.
Farthing, 1920. Includes descents,
pedigrees, list of rectors, biographical
notes, *etc.*

Watton Abbey
See Beverley

Well
HORSFALL, THOMAS. *Notes on the manor of
Well and Snape in the North Riding of
the County of York.* Leeds: J.Whitehead
& Son, 1912. Includes descent of the
manor, memorial inscriptions, notes on
parish records, *etc.*

Wensleydale
HALLAS, CHRISTINE S. 'Migration in
nineteenth-century Wensleydale and
Swaledale', *N.H.* 27, 1991, 139-61. Based on
census materials, *etc.*

Wharfedale
MALTBY, BESSIE. 'Parish registers and the
problem of mobility', *Local population
studies* 6, 1971, 32-42. Study of
Wharfedale parishes, based on parish
register.
LONG, MOIRA, & PICKLES, MAY. 'An enquiry
into mortality in some mid-Wharfedale
parishes in 1623', *Local population studies*
37, 1986, 19-35. Based on parish registers.
PICKLES, MAY F. 'Agrarian society and wealth
in mid-Wharfedale, 1664-1743', *Y.A.J.* 53,
1981, 63-78. Based on probate inventories.
PICKLES, MAY F. 'Mid-Wharfedale, 1721-1812:
economic and demographic change in a
Pennine Dale', *Local population studies*
16, 1976, 12-44. Based primarily on parish
registers.
SPEIGHT, HARRY. *Lower Wharfedale, being a
complete account of the history,
antiquities and scenery of the picturesque
valley of the Wharfe, from Cawood to
Arthington.* Elliot Stock, 1902. Includes
pedigrees, with many notes on families.
SPEIGHT, HARRY. *Upper Wharfedale, being a
complete account of the history,
antiquities and scenery of the picturesque
valley of the Wharfe, from Otley to
Langstrothdale.* Elliot Stock, 1900.
Reprinted Otley: Smith Settle, 1988.
Includes folded pedigrees of Maude of
Burley in Wharfedale, Cavendish, Dukes
of Devonshire, and Tennant of Bordley,
with many notes on families.
See also Leeds

Wharram Percy
ANDREWS, D.D., & MILNE, G. *Wharram: a
study of settlement on the Yorkshire
Wolds. Volume I. Domestic settlement, 1:
areas 10 and 6.* Monograph series **8.**
Society for Medieval Archaeology, 1979.
Includes BERESFORD, M.W. 'Documentary
evidence for the history of Wharram Percy'.
BELL, R.D., BERESFORD, M.W., et al. *Wharram:
a study of settlement on the Yorkshire
Wolds. Volume III. Wharram Percy: the
church of St. Martin.* Monograph series **11.**
Society for Medieval Archaeology, 1987.
Includes chapter on 'the documentary
evidence', including a description of the
parish register.

BERESFORD, MAURICE, & HURST, JOHN. *English heritage book of Wharram Percy: deserted medieval village.* Batsford English Heritage, 1990. Account of a classic archaeological excavation, including discussion of gravestones, and facsimile of a mid-18th c. rental.

Whitby

BARKER, ROSALIN. 'Comparing demographic experience: Harwich and Whitby, 1750-1800', *Local population studies* **46**, 1991, 32-8. Based on parish registers.

CHARLTON, LIONEL. *History of Whitby and of Whitby Abbey, collected from the original records of the abbey, and other authentic memoirs never before made public, containing not only the history of Whitby and the country adjacent, but also the original and antiquity of many particular families and places in other parts of Yorkshire ...* T. Cadell, 1779.

YOUNG, GEORGE. *A history of Whitby and Streoneshalh Abbey, with a statistical survey of the vicinity to the distance of twenty-five miles.* 2 vols. Whitby: Clark and Medd, 1817. Includes chapter on 'biography and family history'.

Whitewell

WHITAKER, THOMAS D. *A history of the original parish of Whalley and the Honour of Clitheroe to which is subjoined an account of the parish of Cartmell.* 4th ed. revised by John Gough Nichols & Ponsonby A. Lyons. 2 vols. George Routledge & Sons, 1872-6. Although Whalley is primarily in Lancashire, it includes Whitewell in Yorkshire. Many pedigrees, extracts from original sources, biographical memoirs, *etc.*

Winestead

MILLER, NORMAN JAMES. *Winestead & its lords: the history of a Holderness village.* Hull: A. Brown & Sons, 1932. Includes account of the Hildyard family, with folded pedigree, 13-19th c.
See also Keyingham

Withernsea

MILES, GEO. T., & RICHARDSON, WILLIAM. *A history of Withernsea with notices of other parishes in South Holderness in the*

East Riding of the County of York. Hull: A. Brown & Sons, 1911. Effectively a parochial survey of South Holderness; many extracts from parish registers.

Woodall
See Harthill

Woodchurch
See Morley

Woolley

WALKER, J.W. 'The manor and church of Woolley', *Y.A.J.* **27**, 1924, 249-318. Includes pedigrees (some folded) of Notton of Notton, 13-16th c., Biri and Wheatley of Woolley, 13-18th c., Dicton, Stainton and Popeley, 13-17th c., Woodrove, 13-18th c., Wentworth, 16-20th c., also heraldic notes, *etc.*

Yarm

WARDELL, JOHN WILFORD. *A history of Yarm, an ancient North Riding town.* Sunderland: the author, 1957. Includes many extracts from original sources, e.g. enclosure award 1658, tithe apportionment, 1838, *etc., etc.*

York

TILLOTT, P.M., ed. *A history of Yorkshire: the City of York.* Oxford University Press for the Institute of Historical Research, 1961. Part of the *Victoria county history* series. Authoritative.

BIGGINS, JAMES M. *Historians of York.* St. Anthony's Hall publications **10**. 1956.

DRAKE, FRANCIS. *Eboracum, or, the history and antiquities of the City of York ...* 2 vols. W. Bowyer for the author, 1736. Reprinted EP Publishing, 1978. Includes plates of many inscriptions, also deeds.

G[ENT], T. *The antient and modern history of the famous City of York, and in a particular manner of its magnificent cathedral, commonly called York Minster, as also an account of St. Mary's Abbey and other antient religious houses and churches ... with a description of those churches now in use, of their curiously painted windows, the inscriptions carefully collected, and many of them translated, the lives of the Archbishops of this see ... an account of the mayors and bayliffs, lord mayors and sheriffs ...* York: Thomas Hammond, 1730.

HARGROVE, WILLIAM. *History and description of the ancient city of York, comprising all the most interesting information already published in Drake's Eboracum, enriched with much entirely new matter from other authentic sources* ... 2 vols. York: Wm. Alexander, 1818. Includes lists of lord mayors, sheriffs and deans, monumental inscriptions, topographical survey, *etc.*

HARVEY, JOHN. *York.* B.T. Batsford, 1975. Historical and topographical description.

PEACOCK, A.J., ed. *Essays in York history.* York: York Settlement Trust, [1997]. Reprint of all 6 volumes of the journal, *York history.*

STACPOOLE, ALBERIC, et al. eds. *The noble City of York.* York: Cerialis Press, 1972. Collection of essays.

TORR, JAMES. *The antiquities of York city, and the civil government thereof, with a list of all the mayors and bayliffs, lord mayors and sheriffs, from the time of King Edward the First, to this present year 1719, collected from the papers of Christopher Hildyard, esq., with notes and observations and the addition of ancient inscriptions and coates of arms, from gravestones and church-windows.* York: G. White for F. Hildyard.

WIDDRINGTON, THOMAS, SIR. *Analecta Eboracensia: some remaynes of the ancient City of York,* ed. Caesar Caine. C.J. Clark, 1897. Includes many extracts from original sources; also pedigree of Widdrington 17th c.

An inventory of the historical monuments in the City of York. 5 vols. H.M.S.O., 1972-81. Contents: v.1. Ebvracum: Roman York; v.2. The defences; v.3. South-West of the Ouse; v.4. Outside the city walls, east of the Ouse; v.5. The central area. These volumes provide authoritative descriptions of houses. Few names are mentioned, but there is an armorial index in v.5.

SAYLES, GEORGE. 'The dissolution of a guild at York in 1306', *English historical review* **55**, 1940, 83-98. Includes transcript of an assize roll with many names.

CULLUM, P.H., & GOLDBERG, P.J.P. 'Charitable provision in late medieval York: 'to the praise of God and the use of the poor', *N.H.* **29**, 1993, 24-39. Based on wills.

DOBSON, BARRIE. 'Citizens and chantries in late medieval York', in ABULAFIA, DAVID,

FRANKLIN, MICHAEL, & RUBIN, MIRI, eds. *Church and city, 1000-1500: essays in honour of Christopher Brooke.* Cambridge: Cambridge University Press, 1992, 311-32. Based on a collection of deeds relating to York charities.

KERMODE, JENNIFER I. 'Urban decline? The flight from office in late medieval York', *Economic history review* **35**, 1982, 179-98. General discussion.

PALLISER, D.M. *Tudor York.* Oxford: Oxford University Press, 1979. Scholarly.

COWGILL, URSULA M. 'Life and death in the sixteenth century in the City of York', *Population studies* **21**, 1967, 53-62. Based on published parish registers.

GALLEY, CHRIS. 'A never ending succession of epidemics? Mortality in early modern York', *Social history of medicine* **7**, 1994, 29-57. Based on parish registers.

COSTER, WILL. 'To bring them up in the fear of God: guardianship in the Diocese of York, 1500-1668', *Continuity & change* **10**, 1995, 9-32. Based on wills from St. Margaret's, York, Bilton in Ainsty, and Almondbury, and also on an act book containing bonds of guardianship, 1592-1638.

GALLEY, CHRIS. *The demography of early modern towns: York in the sixteenth and seventeenth centuries.* Liverpool: Liverpool University Press, 1998. Not seen.

GALLEY, CHRIS. 'A model of early modern urban demography', *Economic history review* 2nd series **48**, 1995, 448-69. Study of York, based on parish registers.

WENHAM, L.P. *The great and close siege of York.* Kineton: Roundwood Press, 1970.

HIBBERD, DEBORAH. 'Data-linkage and the hearth tax: the case of seventeenth-century York', in ALLDRIDGE, N.J., ed. *The hearth tax: problems and possibilities.* Hull: Humberside College of Higher Education, for C.O.R.A.L., 1983, 59-75.

DIGBY, ANNE. *Madness, morality and medicine: a study of the York retreat, 1796-1914.* Cambridge: Cambridge University Press, 1985.

ARMSTRONG, ALAN. *Stability and change in an English county town: a social study of York, 1801-1851.* Cambridge: C.U.P., 1974. Based largely on the census and parish registers.

FEINSTEIN, C.H., ed. *York, 1831-1981: 150 years of scientific endeavour and social change.* York: William Sessions, 1981. Collection of essays.

PEACOCK, A.J. *York in the Great War, 1914 to 1918.* York: York Settlement Trust, [1993]. General history.

HILLS, R.I. *The General Strike in York, 1926.* Borthwick papers **57**. 1980.

3. BIBLIOGRAPHY AND ARCHIVES

A. *Introduction*

This bibliography, although it aims to list all of the most important titles for genealogists, is far from being a complete listing of Yorkshire historical publications. No comprehensive and up to date Yorkshire bibliography is available. There are, however, many bibliographies devoted to specific topics, and these are listed here. Also listed are the profusion of guides to archives which have emanated from record offices, libraries, and family history societies. There are innumerable institutions serving the genealogist in Yorkshire, and it is always useful to check their published guides and handbooks before visiting them.

A brief general survey for genealogists researching in Yorkshire is provided by:

LITTON, PAULINE M. *Basic facts about ... family history research in Yorkshire.* Rev. ed. Birmingham: Federation of Family History Societies, 1997.

A number of surveys of historical writings on the county are printed in:

CURRIE, C.R.J., & LEWIS, C.P., eds. *English county histories: a guide.* Stroud: Alan Sutton, 1994. Includes essays on Yorkshire (by G.C.F. Forster), the East Riding (by G.H.R. Kent), the North Riding and City of York (by W.J. Sheils), and the West Riding (by G.C.F. Forster).

The best general bibliography (although originally published in 1869) is still:

BOYNE, WILLIAM. *The Yorkshire library: a bibliographical account of books on topography, tracts of the seventeenth century, biography, spaws, geology, botany, maps, views, portraits, and miscellaneous literature relating to the County of York, with collations and notes on the books and the authors.* Taylor & Co., 1869. Reprinted Hull: N.T. Leslie, 1974.

Additions to Boyne are listed in:

BARNARD, ROBERT. *Scarce, not in Boyne: a selective catalogue of Hull and East Riding books to 1900.* Hull: Hull College Local History Unit, 1998.

See also:

HAILSTONE, EDWARD. *Catalogue of a collection of historical and topographical works and Civil War Tracts relating to the County of York ... in the library of Edward Hailstone, esq., F.S.A., Lond. and Scot., etc., at Horton Hall.* [ ]: Privately published, 1858.

A number of library catalogues have been published. The most useful is that of the Yorkshire Archaeological Society, which aims to collect all publications on Yorkshire history. It is now over 60 years since this catalogue was compiled, but it remains invaluable for identifying obscure materials published before then. Most items listed are still held by the Society. See:

KIRK, GEORGE E. *Catalogue of the printed books and pamphlets in the library of the Yorkshire Archaeological Society ... 30th November, 1932.* 2 vols. Leeds: the Society, 1935-6.

Other library catalogues include:

Catalogue of books and pamphlets relating to Yorkshire. Bradford: Bradford Public Free Library, 1892. In Bradford Library in 1892; many titles listed.

City of York Public Library: List of books in the local collection relating to the City and County of York. York: Yorkshire Print Co., 1912.

WALTON, MARY. 'The Hunter collection in the Sheffield Central Library', *T. Hunter A.S.* **13**, 1985, 47-64. Catalogue of the Hunter Archaeological Society's library.

'Catalogue of books, engravings, drawings, &c., in the possession of the Thoresby Society', in *Miscellanea* [2]. *T.S.* **4**, 1895, xxv-xxxv.

Numerous periodicals relating to Yorkshire are or have been published. Their contents are listed in:

'Yorkshire bibliography', *Y.A.J.* **28-55**, 1928-83, *passim.* Title and author varies.

Theses are rarely consulted by genealogists. They should be! There are two listings available specific to Yorkshire:

GILBERT, V.F., & HOLMES, C. *Theses and dissertations in economic and social history in Yorkshire universities, 1920-1974.* Sheffield: University Library, 1974.

DYSON, BRIAN. *Theses relating to East Yorkshire and Humberside: a checklist.* Sources for regional and local history 3. Hull: University of Hull Centre for Regional and Local History, 1986.

Other miscellaneous bibliographies include:

BELLAMY, JOYCE M. *Yorkshire business histories: a bibliography.* Bradford University Press, 1970.

EXWOOD, J. ELISABETH, & UNWIN, R.W. *Yorkshire topography: a guide to historical sources and their uses.* Leeds: University of Leeds Institute of Education, 1974.

FIRTH, G., LAYBOURNE, K., & O'CONNELL, J., eds. *Yorkshire labour movements c.1780-1926: a guide to historical sources and their uses.* Leeds: University of Leeds School of Education, [1977?]

CROUCHER, TREVOR. *Boots and books: the work and writings of Arthur Raistrick.* Otley: Smith Settle, 1995.

B. *Local Bibliographies and Lists of Sources*

Numerous bibliographies devoted to specific places are available and should be checked if you have an interest in the locality concerned. There are also many lists of original sources, which are invaluable if you are trying to identify archival sources for a specific place.

Allerton

WILLMOTT, ELVIRA. 'Allerton', *Bod-kin* **2**(2), 1997, 10-14. List of sources.

Barton on Humber

KETCHELL, CHRISTOPHER. *Barton on Humber: a Barton on Humber bibliography. Sources of local history information about Barton on Humber.* Know your place bibliography 11. Hull: Hull College of Further Education, 1990.

Beverley

BROWN, WILLIAM. 'Documents from the Record Office relating to Beverley', *T.E.R.A.S.* **5**, 1897, 35-49. From the patent rolls, *inquisitions ad quod damnum,* and *inquisitions post mortem,* 14th c.

'Spotlight on Beverley', *B.T.* **74**, 1998, 21-4. List of sources.

Bolton

WILLMOTT, ELVIRA. 'Bolton', *Bod-kin* **45**, 1996, 10-14. Township in Calverley parish. List of sources.

Bowling

WILLMOTT, ELVIRA. 'Bowling township', *Bod-kin* **35**, 1994, 12-14; **36**, 1994, 13-14. List of sources.

WILLMOTT, ELVIRA. 'Book list: Bowling', *Bod-kin* **25**, 1991, 20. Brief bibliography.

Bradford

DICKONS, J. NORTON. *A catalogue of books, pamphlets &c., published at Bradford in the County of York.* Bradford: privately printed, 1895.

RUSHWORTH, PHILIP. *Tracing your Bradford ancestors.* Bradford: the author, 1979.

RUSHWORTH, PHILIP. *Retracing your Bradford ancestors.* Bradford: the author, 1984. More detailed than the previous work.

STRONG, R. 'Sources for the history of Bradford metropolitan district', *Y.A.J.* **47**, 1975, 133-6. At the Yorkshire Archaeological Society.

WILLMOTT, ELVIRA. 'Bradford township', *Bod-kin* **30**, 1993, 12-14; **31**, 1993, 10-12; **32**, 1993, 10-11; **33**, 1993, 9-10; **34**, 1994, 9-11. List of sources.

Bridlington

'Spotlight on Bridlington', *B.T.* **70**, 1997, 20-22. Lists sources.

Calderdale

RUSHWORTH, PHILIP. *Tracing your Calderdale ancestors.* Bradford: the author, 1980.

Catwick

'Catwick (material to be found in the Record Office, Beverley)', *B.T.* **8**, 1980/1, 10-11. List of parish records.

Cherry Burton

'Cherry Burton: material to be found in the Record Office, Beverley', *B.T.* **6**, 1980, 19-25. List of parish registers and records; also of names on gravestones.

Clayton

WILLMOTT, ELVIRA. 'Clayton', *Bod-kin* **44**, 1996, 10-14. List of sources.

Cleveland

CUTHBERTSON, ALMA M. *Cleveland bibliography 1974-1983: guide to published items relating to the Cleveland county area during the first ten years of the existence of the local authority.* Middlesbrough: Teesside Polytechnic, 1985. Continued by occasional supplements.

HOWE, J.C. 'Know your parish', *J.Cl.F.H.S.* **6**(8), 1996, 30-31. List of articles in *J.Cl.F.H.S.* on the history of particular parishes, not cited elsewhere in the present volume.

'Cleveland history: a survey of publications', *Cleveland history* **61**- , 1991- , *passim*.

Denholme

WILLMOTT, ELVIRA. 'Denholme', *Bod-kin* **2**(6), 1998, 10-13. List of sources.

Driffield

KETCHELL, CHRISTOPHER. *A Driffield bibliography: sources of information about Driffield.* Know your place local history bibliography 3. Hull: Local History Archives Unit, 1989.

East Ayton

See Seamer

East Riding

DICKENS, A.G., & MACMAHON, K.A. *A guide to regional studies on the East Riding of Yorkshire and the city of Hull.* Hull: University of Hull Departments of Adult Education and History, 1956. Valuable bibliography.

DYSON, BRIAN, ed. *A guide to local studies in East Yorkshire.* Beverley: Hutton Press, 1985. Collection of essays.

ENGLISH, BARBARA. 'Electronic bibliography: an example from East Yorkshire', *Local historian* **19**, 1989, 117-9. Brief description of the East Yorkshire bibliography, which can be accessed on the internet via the University of Hull's site.

CROWTHER, PETER. 'The East Yorkshire bibliography: an update', in CROWTHER, JAN, & CROWTHER, PETER, eds. *Collected articles from the Bulletin of the East Yorkshire Local History Society, nos. 1-55, 1970-Feb. 1997.* [ ]: the Society, 1997, vol. 1, 75. Originally published in the *Bulletin* **43**, 1990-1, 7-8.

Eccleshill
WILLMOTT, ELVIRA 'Eccleshill', *Bod-kin* **28**, 1992, 11-13. List of sources.

Esholt
WILLMOTT, ELVIRA. 'Esholt', *Bod-kin* **2**(5), 1998, 10-13. List of sources.

Flamborough
'Spotlight on Flamborough', *B.T.* **68**, 1996, 17-19. Lists sources.

Goole
KETCHELL, CHRISTOPHER. *A Goole bibliography: sources of local history information about Goole.* Know your place local history bibliography **4**. Hull: Hull College of Further Education Local History Unit, 1989.

Great Driffield
'Spotlight on Great Driffield', *B.T.* **72**, 1997, 13-14.

Heaton
WILLMOTT, ELVIRA. 'Heaton', *Bod-kin* **29**, 1992, 9-11. List of sources.

Hedon
OSTLER, GORDON. *Hedon: a Hedon bibliography: sources of local history information about Hedon.* Know your place bibliography **8**. Hull: Hull College of Further Education Local History Archives Unit, 1990.

Hessle
KETCHELL, CHRISTOPHER. *A Hessle bibliography: sources of local history information about Hessle.* Know your place bibliography **12**. Hull: Hull College of Further Education Local History Unit, 1992.

Hornsea
KETCHELL, CHRISTOPHER. *Hornsea: a Hornsea bibliography: sources of local history information about Hornsea.* Know your place bibliography **14**. Hull: Hull College of Further Education Local History Unit, 1991.
'Spotlight on Hornsea', *B.T.* **76**, 1998, 17-19. Lists sources.

Horton
WILLMOTT, ELVIRA. 'Horton township', *Bod-kin* **37**, 1994, 14-16; **38**, 1995, 11-13; **39**, 1995, 11-12.

Howden
KETCHELL, CHRISTOPHER. *Howden: a Howden bibliography: sources of local history information about Howden.* Know your place bibliography **10**. Hull: Hull College of Further Education Local History Unit, 1992.

Hull
DREWERY, ROBERT FORRESTER. *Books on Hull and district: a select list.* Hull: Kingston upon Hull Public Libraries, 1957.
KETCHELL, CHRISTOPHER. *East Hull: an East Hull bibliography and chronology.* Know your place bibliography **24**. Hull: Hull College Local History Unit, 1995.
KETCHELL, CHRISTOPHER. *A Hessle Road bibliography: sources of information about Hessle Road, Hull.* Know your place bibliography **5**. Hull: Hull College of Further Education Local History Archives Unit, 1989.
KETCHELL, CHRISTOPHER. *I remember: a recall and reminiscence bibliography and local resource directory.* 3rd ed. Local History Archives Unit resource guide **2**. Hull: Hull College of Higher Education, 1988. Listing of oral histories relating to Hull.

Humberside
HUMBERSIDE LIBRARIES. *A select bibliography of the County of Humberside.* [Hull]: Humberside Libraries and Amenities Department, 1980.

Hunmanby
'Spotlight on … Hunmanby', *B.T.* **58**, 1994,
21-7. List of sources, and extract from
Bulmer's 1892 *Directory*.

Idle
WILLMOTT, ELVIRA. 'Idle township', *Bod-kin*
42, 1996, 10-14; 43, 1996, 10-11.

Kirk Ella
'Spotlight on … Kirk Ella', *B.T.* **59**, 1994, 17-
22. Lists various sources, with extract
from Bulmer's 1892 *directory*.

Manningham
WILLMOTT, ELVIRA. 'Manningham Township',
Bod-kin **40**, 1995, 10-14; **41**, 1995, 11-13.
List of sources.

Market Weighton
KETCHELL, CHRISTOPHER. *A Market
Weighton bibliography: sources for the
history of Market Weighton*. Know your
place bibliography **16**. Hull: Hull College
of Further Education Local History Unit,
1992.

North Bierley
WILLMOTT, ELVIRA. 'North Bierley', *Bod-kin*
27, 1992, 12-14. List of sources.

North Newbald
'North Newbald (material to be found in the
Record Office, Beverley)', *B.T.* **7**, 1980, 21-
3. List of parish registers and records; also
of names on gravestones.

North Riding
JEAFFRESON, JOHN CORDY. 'Manuscripts of
the North Riding of Yorkshire', *Y.A.J.* **8**,
1884, 175-8. Brief list.

Patrington
'Spotlight on Patrington', *B.T.* **69**, 1997, 20-
22. Lists sources.

Pocklington
KETCHELL, CHRISTOPHER. *A Pocklington
bibliography: sources of information
about Pocklington*. Know your place local
history bibliography **2**. Hull: Local History
Archives Unit, 1989.

'Spotlight on Pocklington', *B.T.* **73**, 1998, 15-
17. Lists sources.

Pontefract
BRISCOE, GILL. *Pontefract and Wakefield
ancestors: a family historians guide to
sources and where to find them*.
Pontefract: Pontefract & District F.H.S.,
[1999?]

Queensberry
WILLMOTT, ELVIRA. 'Queensberry', *Bod-kin*
2(4), 1997, 10-15. List of sources.

Ripon
HEBDEN, BRIAN. *A guide to historical
sources for Ripon and district*. Ripon:
Ripon Historical Society/Ripon, Harrogate
& District Family History Group, 1994.
Extensive listing of primary sources by
record office, also good bibliography.

Rudston
'Spotlight on Rudston', *B.T.* **77**, 1999, 27-8.
Lists sources.

Saddleworth
BARROW, NEIL. 'A Saddleworth bibliography,
1980-89', *B.S.H.S.* **22**(2), 1992, 12-13.

Seamer
'Spotlight on Seamer with East Ayton', *B.T.*
65, 1996, 13-15. Includes list of sources.

Sheffield
CURTIS, E. *Short bibliography of the history
of Sheffield*. Leaflet **25**. Historical
Association, 1911. Brief.
FREEMANTLE, W.T. *A bibliography of
Sheffield and its vicinity to the end of
1700*. Simpkin Marshall Hamilton Kent &
Co., 1911. Includes biographical notes on
authors.
ODOM, W. 'A bibliography of Sheffield
history', *T. Hunter A.S.* **4**, 1937, 85-98.
PYBUS, SYLVIA M. *Basic books on Sheffield
history*. Sheffield: Sheffield City Libraries,
1975. Pamphlet.

Shipley
WILLMOTT, ELVIRA. 'Shipley', *Bod-kin* 2(8),
1998, 10-14; 3(1), 1999, 10-13. List of
sources.

South Cave
'Spotlight on South Cave', *B.T.* **66**, 1996, 21-2. List of sources.

South Yorkshire
Family history in South Yorkshire: a guide to sources. Rotherham: Department of Libraries, Museums & Arts, 1991. Lists record offices, parish registers, monumental inscriptions, cemetery registers, census indexes, directories, electoral registers, *etc.*

Spurn
KETCHELL, CHRISTOPHER. *A Spurn bibliography: sources of local history information about Spurn.* Know your place bibliography **17**. Hull: Hull College of Further Education Local History Unit, 1992.

Sunk Island
KETCHELL, CHRISTOPHER. *Sunk Island: a Sunk Island bibliography: sources for the study of the history of Sunk Island.* Know your place bibliography **18**. Hull: Hull College of Further Education Local History Unit, 1992.

Sutton
CASSIDY, PATRICIA. *Sutton: a Sutton bibliography. Sources of local history information about Sutton on Hull.* Know your place bibliography **9**. Hull: Hull College of Further Education Local History Unit, 1991.
'Spotlight on ... Sutton', *B.T.* **57**, 1994, 19-24. List of sources, with extract from Bulmer's 1892 *directory.*

Swine
KETCHELL, CHRISTOPHER. *Swine: a Swine bibliography: sources for the history of Swine.* Know your place bibliography **23**. Hull: Local History Unit, 1993.

Thornton
WILLMOTT, ELVIRA. 'Thornton', *Bod-kin* **26**, 1992, 12-13. Brief historical note, with useful list of records and books.

Tong
WILLMOTT, ELVIRA. 'Tong', *Bod-kin* 2(3), 1997, 10-14. List of sources.

Wakefield
FEDERER, CHARLES E. *A catalogue of the library of Wakefield books in the possession of Charles Skidmore ...* Privately printed, 1897.
SPEAK, HAROLD. *Wakefield and district: a local studies handlist.* Wakefield: Wakefield Historical Society, 1969. Bibliography.

Wetwang
'Spotlight on Wetwang', *B.T.* **78**, 1999, 27-8. Lists sources.

Wharfedale
MERRIDEW, STANLEY. *Whereabouts of Wharfedale records.* [Leeds]: Wharfedale Family History Group, 1993. List of records by place, giving locations.

Wilsden
WILLMOTT, ELVIRA. 'Wilsden', *Bod-kin* 10-14. List of sources.

Windhill
WILLMOTT, ELVIRA. 'Windhill and Wrose', *Bod-kin* **43**, 1996, 12-15. List of sources.

Withernsea
COOKSON, DAVID. *Withernsea: a Withernsea bibliography: sources of local information about Withernsea.* Know your place local history bibliography **6**. Hull: Hull College of Further Education Local History Archives Unit, 1990.

Withernwick
WOULD, S.O. 'Spotlight on Withernwick', *B.T.* **63**, 1995, 16-19. Includes list of sources.

Wrose
See Windhill

Wyke
WILLMOTT, ELVIRA. 'Wyke', *Bod-kin* 2(1), 1997, 10-14. Township in Birstall. List of sources.

York
MURRAY, HUGH. 'A York bibliography', *York historian* **12**, 1995, 82-7; **13**, 1996, 62-71. Books on York published since 1980.
'Sources in York Reference Library', *C.Y.D.F.H.S.J.* **41**, 1997, 20. Brief list.

C. Archives and Record Offices

There are numerous record offices in Yorkshire; they are listed in:

SOUTHWICK, MICHAEL. *Yorkshire repositories: record holdings in the old historic county for local & family historians.* Winlaton: Kingpin, 1999. This volume also provides summary information on holdings.

Parish records are to be found in many repositories. They may be located by consulting:

BELT, ANN, ed. *Whereabouts of Yorkshire parish records.* Occasional paper **2.** 2 vols. Leeds: Y.A.S., F.H.P.S.S., 1986.

Accessions to many Yorkshire record offices are listed in:

'Archive accessions', *N.H.* **1-14**, 1966-78, *passim.*

The archives accumulated by businesses include much material that could be of genealogical use — personnel records, title deeds, correspondence, *etc., etc.* Records of the wool textile industry, which dominated the West Riding, are listed extensively in:

HUDSON, PATRICIA. *The West Riding wool textile industry: a catalogue of business records from the sixteenth to the twentieth centuries.* Edington: Pasold Research Fund, 1975.

For a general discussion of West Riding business archives, see:

HUDSON, PAT. 'An evaluation of archives relating to West Riding woollen and worsted industries', *Business archives* **37**, 1972, 23-6.

Borthwick Institute

The Borthwick Institute houses the records of the Diocese of York. The *guide* to its collection, originally published in 1973, now has two supplements.

SMITH, DAVID M. *A guide to the archive collections in the Borthwick Institute of Historical Research.* B.T.C. **1.** York: Bk.I.H.R., 1973. See also: 'First supplement to the *Guide to the archive collections',* *B.I.B.* **1**, 1975-8, 11-15.

SMITH, DAVID M. *A supplementary guide to the archive collections in the Borthwick Institute of Historical Research.* B.T.C. **7.** York: Bk.I.H.R., 1980.

BUCHANAN, ALEXANDRINA. *A guide to archival accessions at the Borthwick Institute, 1981-1996.* Borthwick lists and index **19.** York: Borthwick Institute, 1997. Includes many biographical notes on persons mentioned.

See also:

GURNEY, NORAH K.M. 'The Borthwick Institute of Historical Research', *Archives* **7**, 1965-6, 157-62. General discussion of its role, now very dated.

PURVIS, J.S. *The archives of York Diocesan registry.* St.Anthony's Hall Publications **2.** St.Anthony's Press, 1952.

PURVIS, J.S. 'The Borthwick Institute of Historical Research, York', *Transactions of the Ancient Monuments Society* N.S., **1**, 1953, 96-9. Brief; now very dated.

SMITH, DAVID M. 'Archives of genealogical interest at the Borthwick Institute, York', *Genealogists' magazine* **18**, 1975-6, 7-13 & 83-7. Pt.1. Parish and probate records. Pt.2. Legal and clergy records. Originally delivered as a lecture.

WEBB, C.C. *A guide to genealogical sources in the Borthwick Institute of Historical Research.* York: Borthwick Institute, 1981. Description of a wide variety of sources for Yorkshire.

WEBB, C.C. *A guide to parish records in the Borthwick Institute of Historical Research.* B.T.C. **12.** York: Bk.I.H.R., 1987. Lists parish records for the Archdeaconry of York, which covered the West Riding and a few parishes elsewhere.

'The Institute's microfilm library', *B.I.B.* **1**, 1975-8, 128-34. Lists microfilmed original sources held mainly in other repositories.

'Annual report', *B.I.B.* **1-4**, 1975-87, *passim.*

Yorkshire Archaeological Society

For many years, this was the only county-wide archive repository, and it has a particularly valuable collection of estate archives (including the extensive Wakefield manorial rolls). Its holdings are listed in:

CROSSLEY, E.W. *Catalogue of manuscripts and deeds in the library of the Yorkshire Archaeological Society, 1867-1931.* 2nd ed. Wakefield: Archive Advisory Council for West Yorkshire, 1986. Originally published Leeds: Y.A.S., 1931.

THOMAS, S. *Guide to the archive collections of the Yorkshire Archaeological Society, 1931-1983, and the collections deposited with the Society.* Wakefield: Archive Advisory Council for West Yorkshire, 1985. Includes listings of parish register and monumental inscription transcripts. See also:
THOMAS, SYLVIA. 'The archives of the Yorkshire Archaeological Society', *Y.A.J.* **56**, 1984, 1-16. Lecture.
THOMAS, SYLVIA. 'The Yorkshire Archaeological Society', *Local historian* **19**(4), 1989, 170-73. Brief description.
SMITH, MARGARET. 'An industrial history index', *Y.A.J.* **57**, 1985, 189-202. Lists archives relating to industrial history at the Yorkshire Archaeological Society.
PAYNE, BRIAN, & PAYNE, DOROTHY. *Claremont, Leeds.* Leeds: Yorkshire Archaeological Society, 1980. Includes a brief history of the house and its occupants (especially the Heaton family); also a brief account of the Yorkshire Archaeological Society (the present occupier), its archives and library.

St. Mary's Tower, York
Many records were stored in this repository when it was blown up in 1644, but some survive. For a general discussion, see:
ENGLISH, B.A., & BARR, C.B.L. 'The records formerly in St. Mary's Tower, York', *Y.A.J.* **42**, 1971, 198-235, 359-486 & 465-515. The appendices include extensive biographical notes on various record keepers, *etc.*, 16-18th c.
Supplemented by:
ENGLISH, BARBARA, & HOYLE, RICHARD. 'What was in St. Mary's Tower: an inventory of 1610', *Y.A.J.* **65**, 1993, 91-4. List of archives destroyed in 1644. See also:
'Yorkshire monastic archives', *Bodleian quarterly record* **8**(87) 1935, 95-100. Discussion of missing deeds supposedly saved at the destruction of St. Mary's Tower in 1644.

Barnsley Library
BARNSLEY LIBRARY SERVICE. *Family history handbook.* Barnsley: Barnsley Library

Service, 1990. List of registers, enclosure and tithe awards, directories, newspapers *etc.*, held (many on microfilm).

Bradford Archives
Bradford Archives, 1974-1995: an illustrated guide to Bradford District Archives. Wakefield: West Yorkshire Archive Service, 1996.
MASON, IAN. 'News from the archives', *B.A.* 3rd series **3**, 1987, 63-6; **4**, 1989, 78-9; **5**, 1990, 78-81; **6**, 1992, 48-50. Bradford archives accessions, *etc.*
JAMES, DAVID. 'Bradford Archives Department', *B.A.* 3rd series **1**, 1985, 1-10.

Bradford Library
WILLMOTT, ELVIRA. 'Family history and Bradford Public Library', *B.A.* 3rd series **3**, 1987, 58-62.

Calderdale
TURNER, J.BERYL. *Family history research facilities in Cleveland, North Yorkshire and South Durham.* Potto: the author, 1997. Not seen.

Calderdale District Archives
Calderdale archives 1964-1989: an illustrated guide to Calderdale District Archives. Wakefield: West Yorkshire Archive Service, 1990.
'Calderdale District Archives: archive accessions', *T. Hal.A.S.* N.S., **1-** , 1993-, *passim.*

Calderdale Libraries
'Calderdale Libraries welcome the family historian', *Y.F.H.* **21**(2), 1995, 49-50. Brief description of resources.

Cleveland District Archives
Cleveland County Archives Department: genealogical sources. Middlesbrough: the Dept., 1981. Lists archives.
'Sources for genealogical study in the Cleveland County Archives Department, I', *J.Cl.F.H.S.* **1**(1), 1980, 4-7; **1**(2), 1980, 40-43. Lists a wide variety of sources relating to both northern Yorkshire and Co. Durham.
'Transcripts and indexes in Cleveland Archives Dept.', *J.Cl.F.H.S.* **2**(11), 1985, 21-4. Includes parish registers, monumental inscriptions, rolls of honour, *etc., etc.*

TYRELL, D. 'Some recent accessions to the Cleveland County Libraries, Archives Dept.', *C.T.L.H.S.B.* **30**, 1975/6, 64-5.

Conisbrough Local History Society

'Conisbrough Local History Society: contents of the archive, December 1981', *Don. Anc.* **1**(3), 1981, 109-12. A local history society's collection listed.

Cusworth Hall Museum

GOODCHILD, JOHN. *Cusworth Hall Museum: a summary list of the archives in the Museum collection.* Publication 4. [ ]: Doncaster Rural District Council, 1969. Mainly listing business, local government, political and ecclesiastical archives, *etc.*

Doncaster Archives

Guide to the Doncaster Archives Department: diocesan record office for the Archdeaconry of Doncaster. 2nd ed. Doncaster: Doncaster Metropolitan Borough Council, 1981.

BARBER, B. 'A guide to the Archives service', *Don. Anc.* **3**(4), 1987, 113-5. Brief note on Doncaster Archives Dept.

BARBER, BRIAN. 'Doncaster Archives and family history', *Don. Anc.* **9**(3), 1998, 57-9. Brief note.

'Recent accessions in the Doncaster Archives Department', *Don. Anc., passim.*

MACQUIBAN, TIM. 'Name indexes in Doncaster Archives Department', *Don. Anc.* **1**(3), 1981, 57. Brief note.

Hull College Local History Unit

KETCHELL, CHRISTOPHER. *The local guide: guide to sources of local history information in the Local History Unit, Hull College.* 3rd ed. Hull: the Unit, 1996.

KETCHELL, CHRISTOPHER. 'A little local history: a brief history of the Local History Unit, Hull College', *East Yorkshire Local History Society bulletin* **59**, 1998/9, 29-45. Discussion of an unusual institution promoting historical studies in Hull.

Hull Record Office

Guide to the Kingston upon Hull Record Office. Part I. The records of local authorities whose areas or functions were taken over by the former County Borough of Kingston upon Hull. Hull: City Record Office, [1978?]

OXLEY, G.W. *World War II.* Subject guide 1. Hull: Kingston upon Hull City Council, 1980. Brief list of local War records, e.g. casualty lists, personnel registers, *etc.*

Hull University. Brynmore Jones Library

DYSON, BRIAN. 'Archive collections in the Brynmore Jones Library, University of Hull', in CROWTHER, JAN, & CROWTHER, PETER, eds. *Collected articles from the Bulletin of the East Yorkshire Local History Society, nos 1-55, 1970-Feb. 1997.* [ ]: the Society, 1997, vol.1, 81-3. Originally published in the *Bulletin* **33**, 1985/6, 9-13.

DYSON, BRIAN. 'The Hull University Manuscripts and Archives Database', in CROWTHER, JAN, & CROWTHER, PETER, eds. *Collected articles from the Bulletin of the East Yorkshire Local History Society, nos. 1-55, 1970-Feb. 1997.* [ ]: the Society, 1997, vol. 1, 84-5. Originally published in the *Bulletin* **44**, 1991, 14-15.

DYSON, BRIAN. 'What's new on HUMAD2?' *East Yorkshire Local History Society bulletin* **58**, 1998, 22-6.

DYSON, BRIAN, & ROBERTS, HELEN. 'Northern riches: archives and manuscripts in the University of Hull Brynmor Jones Library, *Archives* **22**(96), 1997, 3-14. General description; the collection includes estate archives of over thirty Yorkshire families; also various business, trade union, and ecclesiastical records, *etc.*

Hunter Archaeological Society

SHORT, C.M. 'The archives of the Hunter Archaeological Society', *T. Hunter A.S.* **13**, 1985, 65-6. Brief description.

Keighley Reference Library

PARKER, IRENE. 'Keighley Reference Library: some important sources for family history', *K.D.F.H.S.J.* Summer 1992, 22-3. 'Keighley Reference Library archives', *K.D.F.H.S.J.* Spring 1992, 19. Additions to list in previous article.

Kirklees Archives

Kirklees Archives, 1959-1989: an illustrated guide to Kirklees District Archives. Wakefield: West Yorkshire Archives and Archaeology Joint Committee, 1989.

42

Leeds District Archives
Leeds archives: an illustrated guide to Leeds District Archives. Wakefield: West Yorkshire Archives and Archaeology Joint Committee, 1988.
COLLINSON, J.M. 'The Leeds Archives Department', *N.H.* **15**, 1979, 210-21.

Leeds City Library
SMITH, SANDRA. 'Leeds City Libraries: local and family history library; family history resources and services', *Y.F.H.* **21**(3), 1995, 76-8. Brief description of resources.

North Yorkshire County Record Office
North Riding Record Office report. 1966-73. Annual; includes accessions.
'Records deposited presented and purchased', *Journal* **1**; N.Y.C.R.O.P. **1**, 1975, 6-17.
'North Riding of Yorkshire County Record Office', *J.Cl.F.H.S.* **1**(5), 1981, 119-20. Brief list of sources at Northallerton.

Ripon College
'Local history microfilms held in Ripon College Library', *R.H.* **3**(1), 1996, 26. Brief list.
'Ripon records on microfilm held in the library of the College of Ripon and York St. John', *R.H.* **1**(7), 1992, 6.

Rotherham Archives
'Additions to the archives in 1990', *F.S.* **11**(4), 1991, 91-3. List for Rotherham and Sheffield City Archives.

Sheffield Archives
Guide to the manuscript collections in the Sheffield City Libraries. Sheffield: Libraries, Art Galleries and Museums Committee, 1956.
MEREDITH, ROSAMUND. *Sheffield City Libraries guide to the manuscript collections. Supplement 1956-1976 (superseding previous supplements).* Sheffield: Sheffield City Libraries, 1977.
MEREDITH, R. 'Sheffield City Libraries Archives Department', *N.H.* **9**, 1974, 139-52.
A handlist of records relating to politics in Sheffield, 1832-1980. Sheffield: Sheffield City Libraries, 1982. Lists records of trade unions, M.P.s, councillors, political parties, etc.

POSTLES, D.A. 'List of Sheffield City Libraries Archives Division accessions', *T. Hunter A.S.* **10**(4)-**17**, 1977-93, *passim.*
SHEFFIELD CITY LIBRARIES. *Catalogue of business and industrial records.* Sheffield: Sheffield City Libraries, 1976.

Wakefield District Archives
Wakefield District Archives: a handlist for students. Part one: manuscripts relating to local social life. Archives publication **3**. Wakefield: Wakefield Metropolitan District Libraries, [1981?]

West Yorkshire Archive Service
Guide to the County Record Office for family historians. [Wakefield]: West Yorkshire Metropolitan County Council, c.1983. Notes on a wide range of sources, with listing of parish registers.
BERRY, ELIZABETH. 'The West Yorkshire Archive Service: the development of a unified service 1974-1983, and its work to 1986', *Journal of the Society of Archivists* **8**(4), 1987, 247-57. General discussion of the service, rather than a description of its holdings.
THOMAS, SYLVIA. 'The West Yorkshire Archive Service', *N.H.* **23**, 1987, 194-212. General description of archives at Wakefield, Bradford, Leeds, Halifax and Huddersfield.
JEAFFRESON, JOHN CORDY. 'Manuscripts of the West Riding of Yorkshire', *Y.A.J.* **8**, 1884, 163-74. Brief list of county muniments; includes extracts from early indictment and order books, and schedule of landed Roman Catholics in the Riding between 1717 and 1734.
'West Yorkshire Archive Service', *Y.F.H.* **12**(5), 1986, 110-12. Lists recent accessions.

York
PURVIS, J.S. 'The archives of York', *Studies in church history* **4**, 1967, 1-14. Brief description of the major collections in York, including that at the Borthwick Institute.

York Reference Library
BOWLING, R.G. *Researching family history in York Reference Library.* 4th ed. York: North Yorkshire County Library, 1994.

D. Antiquaries' Collections

Cooke

JEAFFRESON, JOHN CORDY. 'The manuscripts of Philip Bryan Davies Cooke, esquire, of Owston, Co.York, and Gwysaney, Co.Flint, North Wales', in *Sixth report of the Royal Commission on Historical Manuscripts. Part 1. Report and appendix.* H.M.S.O., 1877, 418-26. Brief description of an antiquary's collection, mainly relating to Wales, but with some Yorkshire material.

Dodsworth

MARGERISON, SAML. 'The Dodsworth mss', *Old Yorkshire* 3, 1882, 181-5. List of manuscripts of Yorkshire interest in a major British Library collection.

DENHOLM-YOUNG, N., & CRASTER, H.H.E. 'Roger Dodsworth (1585-1654) and his circle', *Y.A.J.* 32, 1936, 5-32. Description of some manuscript collections of antiquaries.

HOLMES, RICHARD. 'Dodsworth's Yorkshire notes: Wapentake of Osgoldcross', *Y.A.J.* 10, 1887, 250-65, 345-76 & 523-42; 11, 1891, 30-75 & 432-61; 12, 1893, 42-77; 13, 1895, 99-152. Includes folded pedigree of de Lascie, 12-13th c.

'Dodsworth's Yorkshire notes', *Y.A.J.* 6, 1881, 425-50; 7, 1882, 119-41, 259-83 & 401-28; 8, 1884, 1-29 & 481-522. Agbrigg Wapentake; includes extracts from inscriptions, pedigrees, rentals, *etc., etc.*

Goodchild

'The John Goodchild collection', *Yorkshire history quarterly* 1(1), 1995, 19-20. Brief description of a major personal collection of Yorkshire archival materials.

Hopkinson

HORWOOD, ALFRED J. 'The manuscripts of Matthew Wilson, esq., at Eshton Hall, CO. York', in *Third report of the Royal Commission on Historical Manuscripts.* H.M.S.O., 1872, 293-300. Calendar of the Hopkinson manuscripts; John Hopkinson was secretary to Sir William Dugdale, the herald, during his visitation of Yorkshire, and his manuscripts contain much of interest on Yorkshire genealogy, history and topography.

Johnston

CROSSLEY, E.W. 'The mss. of Nathaniel Johnston, M.D., of Pontefract', *Y.A.J.* 32, 1936, 429-41. Antiquary's collection.

HORWOOD, A.J. 'The manuscripts of F.Bacon Frank, esq., of Campsall Hall, Co.York', in *Sixth report of the Royal Commission on Historical Manuscripts. Part 1. Report and appendix.* H.M.S.O., 1877, 448-65. Lists the antiquarian collections of Nathaniel Johnston and R. Frank, both collected for a history of Yorkshire; Johnston attended some of Sir William Dugdale's heraldic visitations.

Lansdowne

MARGERISON, S. 'Yorkshire manuscripts: the Lansdowne mss', *Old Yorkshire* 3, 1882, 174-181. List of manuscripts with Yorkshire content in a major British Library collection.

Nuttall

ROBINSON, LILIAN. 'Barbara Nuttall's papers', *Y.A.S. Local History Study Section bulletin* 32, 1991, 6. Brief list of the note books of a family and local historian; families mentioned include Foljambe, Savile, Sicklemore and Shuttleworth.

Smith

ROBINSON, LILIAN. 'The T.K. Smith collection [Y.A.S. ms. 15171]', *Y.A.S. Local History Study Section bulletin* 33, 1992, 6. Lists collection of local historical notes on Keighley.

Speight

MILNER, H. '[Speight collection at Bradford Library]', *Y.A.S., F.H.P.S.S.N.* 5, 1973, 6-7. List of names from deeds.

Sykes

WHITEHEAD, BARBARA. 'Doctor Sykes papers at Doncaster', *Y.F.H.S.N.* 6, 1982, 3-4. Brief discussion of an antiquary's collection at Doncaster Archives.

Thoresby

LUMB, G.D. 'Mss. written or possessed by Ralph Thoresby F.R.S.', in *Miscellanea* [9]. *T.S.* 28, 1928, 431-63. Letters, notes, *etc.* including list of Leeds (?) taxpayers in 1692.

Towneley

KNOWLES, R.B. 'The manuscripts of Colenel Towneley at Towneley Hall, Burnley', in *Fourth report of the Royal Commission on Historical Manuscripts.* H.M.S.O., 1874, 406-17. Calendar of Christopher Towneley's collections relating to Lancashire and Yorkshire.

E. *Family History Societies*

Family history societies provide invaluable resources for genealogists, and the contents of their journals and newsletters are listed extensively in the present work. In this section, the journals themselves are listed, as are the various directories of genealogists' interests. The latter tend to be issued every two or three years, and it is always worth checking whether later editions are available than those cited here.

For brief descriptions of 16 societies, now rather dated, see:
JEPSON, DAVID T. *Yorkshire family history societies.* [ ]: Federation of Family History Societies, 1994.
British Isles genealogical register 1997. Fiche. Federation of Family History Societies, 1997. New edition in preparation.
PERKINS, JOHN. *Yorkshire families directory 4.* 2 vols. Federation of Family History Societies (North East Region), 1991. Earlier issues may also be useful, although now out of date.

Barnsley Family History Society
Barnsley Family History Society newsletter. 1990-92. Continued by: *Barnsley Family History Society journal.* 1993- .

Bradford Family History Society
The Bod-kin: Bradford Family History Society newsletter. 1985- .
BRADFORD FAMILY HISTORY SOCIETY. *Members' interests directory no. 2.* Bradford: Bradford F.H.S., 1993.

Calderdale Family History Society
The Scrivenor: the journal of the Calderdale Family History Society. [1988- .]? Earliest issues not seen.

Cleveland Family History Society
The Journal of Cleveland Family History Society. 1980- .

PERKINS, JOHN P. *Cleveland Family History Society members' interests 1989-90.* Redcar: Cleveland F.H.S., 1989.

Doncaster & District Family History Society
'Guest society: Doncaster & District Family History Society', *Family Tree Magazine* 9(3), 1993, 19.
The Doncaster ancestor: the journal of the Doncaster Society for Family History. 1980- . The society changed its name to Doncaster and District Family History Society from v.5, no.3, 1992.
Doncaster & District Family History Society members' interests 1992. Doncaster: Doncaster & District F.H.S., 1992.

East Yorkshire Family History Society
CAWLEY, ANDREA. 'East Yorkshire Family History Society', *Family tree magazine* 2(3), 1986, 22.
The Banyan tree: journal of the East Yorkshire Family History Society. 1977- .
East Yorkshire Family History Society members' interests, 1998. [ ]: E.Y.F.H.S., 1998. Also available on fiche. Earlier issues may also be useful.

Huddersfield & District Family History Society
WHITWAM, STEPHEN D. 'Huddersfield & District Family History Society', *Family tree magazine* 8(5), 1992, 40.
Huddersfield & District Family History Society journal. 1987- .
'Index of articles in vols. 1/1 to 4/3', *H. & D.F.H.S.J.* 4(4), 1991, 118-9.

Keighley & District Family History Society
Keighley & District Family History Society journal. [1989?]- . Earliest issues not seen.
KEIGHLEY & DISTRICT FAMILY HISTORY SOCIETY. *Members' Interests 1994* Keighley: The Society, 1994.

Morley & District Family History Group
The Cameo: Morley & District Family History Group newsletter. 1989- .

Pontefract & District Family History Society

The Bridge: journal of the Pontefract & District Family History Society. 1997- .

Parishes covered by Pontefract and Disrict Family History Society. Pontefract: the Society, [1999?] Brief descriptions of parishes and townships covered, from Baines' *Directory,* 1823.

Ripon Historical Society/Ripon, Harrogate & District Family History Group

The Ripon historian: the journal of the Ripon Historical Society and Ripon Harrogate & District Family History Group. 1988- . Sub-title varies. Indexed in: 'Ripon Historian: index to volume one, numbers 1-10', *R.H.* 2(1), 1993, 9-14.

Rotherham & District Family History Society

Rotherham and District Family History Society [newsletter]. 1984-7.

Sheffield & District Family History Society

The flowing stream: journal of the Sheffield and District Family History Society. 1977- .

Wakefield & District Family History Society

Wakefield & District Family History Society journal. 1997-8. Continued as *Wakefield kinsman.* 1999- .

WAKEFIELD & DISTRICT FAMILY HISTORY SOCIETY. *Directory of Members' interests, September 1997.* Wakefield: The Society, 1997.

Wharfedale Family History Group

MERRIDEW, STANLEY. 'The Wharfedale Family History Group', *Family tree magazine* 11(7), 1995, 53.

Wharfedale newsletter: the journal of the Wharfedale Family History Group. 1990- .

City of York & District Family History Society

York Family History Society newsletter. 1980-87. Continued as *The City of York and District Family History Society newsletter.* 1988-95, and as *The City of York & District Family History Society journal.* 1996- .

Yorkshire Archaeological Society Family History and Population Studies Section

RAYNER, J. 'Guest society: the Family History and Population Studies Section of the Yorkshire Archaeological Society', *Family tree magazine* 13(2), 1996, 49.

The Yorkshire Archaeological Society Family History and Population Studies Section newsletter. 1973-84. Continued by: *Yorkshire family historian.* 1985- . Indexed in:

Yorkshire family historian index 1973-1992. 1 fiche. Leeds: Y.A.S., F.H.P.S.S., 1992.

Members' directory of the Family History and Population Studies Section, Yorkshire Archaeological Society. Leeds: Y.A.S., F.H.P.S.S., 1975.

4. JOURNALS AND NEWSPAPERS

Family history society newsletters and journals are listed in section 3(D) above. There are many other historical journals of relevance to the genealogist, and numerous articles from them are listed in the appropriate places in this bibliography. The major county-wide journal is:
The Yorkshire archaeological and topographical journal. Yorkshire Archaeological Society, 1870- . Now the *Yorkshire archaeological journal.* A number of indexes to this journal are available:
'An index to the *Yorkshire archaeological journal* volumes 1-52 (1870-1980) and to certain other publications of the Society', *Y.A.J.* **53**, 1981, 163-84.
LAWRANCE, HENRY. *Analytical index of the contents of the first thirty volumes of the Society's journal.* Leeds: Yorkshire Archaeological Society, 1939.
FOSTER, AMY G. *Analytical index of the contents of the Yorkshire archaeological journal, volumes XXXI-XL, 1934-1962.* Leeds: Y.A.S., 1963.
WHITAKER, ARTHUR H. *Analytical index of the contents of volumes XLI-LXII of the 'Yorkshire archaeological journal', together with the 'Yorkshire archaeological register', 1989.* Leeds: Y.A.S., 1990.
BUTLER, R.M. 'An index to the *Yorkshire archaeological journal,* volumes 53-60, and to certain other publications of the Society', *Y.A.J.* **61**, 1989, 207-8.
The Yorkshire Archaeological Society has a number of sections, some of which publish their own bulletins *etc.* (including a family history & population studies section, for which see above). The bulletin of the Local History Study Section has included a number of articles relevant to the genealogist:
Yorkshire Archaeological Society Local History Study Section bulletin. [197-?] — . Title varies; became *Bulletin* from **32**, 1993. Earliest issues not seen. Indexed in:
'The L.H.S.S. bulletin: its origins and a list of published articles', *Y.A.S. Local History Study Section bulletin* **34**, 1993, 4-6.

Another major journal, carrying wide-ranging, scholarly articles relating to the history of the north of England as a whole is:
Northern history: a review of the history of the North of England. Leeds: University of Leeds School of History, 1966- .
For a useful series of short monographs, see:
St. Anthony's Hall publications. 26 vols. St. Anthony's Press, 1953-64. Continued as: *Borthwick papers.* 1964- .
Record society publications relating to Yorkshire are numerous, and many are listed in appropriate places in this bibliography. Full listings of two major series are available, although they are now rather out of date:
CLAY, CHARLES TRAVIS. *A catalogue of the publications of the record series 1885-1946, with an introductory chapter on its history.* Y.A.S., R.S. **113**. 1948.
THOMPSON, A. HAMILTON. *The Surtees Society, 1834-1934, including a catalogue of its publications, with notes on their sources and contents, and a list of the members of the society from its beginning to the present day.* Surtees Society **150**. 1935. The Surtees Society also publishes sources for a number of other northern counties.
These listings may be supplemented by:
MULLINS, E.L.C. *Texts and calendars: an analytical guide to serial publications.* Royal Historical Society guides & handbooks **7**. 1978. A supplement (guides & handbooks **12**) covers publications from 1974 to 1982, and subsequent material is listed on the internet at http://www.hmc.gov.uk/socs/list.htm.
SMITH, DAVID M. 'Archives of genealogical interest at the Borthwick Institute, York', *Genealogists' magazine* **18**, 1975-6, 7-13 & 83-7. Pt.1. Parish and probate records. Pt.2. Legal and clergy records. Originally delivered as a lecture.
A specifically genealogical journal, covering Durham and Northumberland as well as Yorkshire, is:
The North-Easterner. Winlaton: Kingpin, 1994- .

There are or have been quite a number of other county-wide journals, listed here by date of commencement. Care needs to be taken to distinguish between those which have similar titles.

Old Yorkshire. Longman Green & Co., 1881-91. 8 vols.

Yorkshire notes and queries, with the Yorkshire genealogist, Yorkshire bibliographer and Yorkshire folk-lore journal. Bingley: T. Harrison for J. Horsfall Turner, 1888-90.

Yorkshire genealogist. 2 vols. Bingley: J. Horsfall Turner, 1888-90. v.2. incorporates *Yorkshire bibliographer.* Continued by:

Yorkshire county magazine, with which are incorporated the Yorkshire notes & queries, Yorkshire folk-lore journal, Yorkshire genealogist, and Yorkshire bibliographer. 4 vols. Bingley: T. Harrison & Sons, 1891-4.

Notes and queries: a quarterly magazine (illustrated) devoted to the antiquities, family traditions, parochial records, folk lore, quaint customs, etc., of South Yorkshire, Derbyshire, Notts., and Lincolnshire. 2 vols. Sheffield: Sir W.C. Lengard Co., 1899-1900. Not to be confused with the national journal of the same title.

Yorkshire notes and queries, being the antiquarian history of Yorkshire. 5 vols. Bradford: Henry Casaubon-Derwent, 1905-9.

Borthwick Institute bulletin. 1975-87. Ceased with 4(1).

Old West Riding. Huddersfield: Greenhead Books, 1981- . Brief articles.

Yorkshire history quarterly. Settle: Hudson History, 1995- .

Bradford

The Bradford antiquary: the journal of the Bradford Historical and Antiquarian Society. 1888- .

Cleveland & Teesside

Cleveland and Teesside Local History Society bulletin. 1968-91. Continued by *Cleveland history: the bulletin of the Cleveland and Teesside Local History Society.* 1991- .

Cottingham

The Cottingham Local History Society journal. 1954- .

Doncaster

Yesterday today: Doncaster's local history quarterly review. Doncaster: Doncaster Libraries, 1991- . Mainly notes on current historical activities.

East Riding

The transactions of the East Riding Antiquarian Society. 1893-1953. Indexed in:

COX, J. CHARLES. *Index to the first twenty volumes of the Transactions.* Hull: East Riding Archaeological Society, 1919.

The East Yorkshire Local History Society bulletin. 1970- . News and lists of new books and theses appear in most issues. More substantial articles have been reprinted in:

CROWTHER, JAN, & CROWTHER, PETER, eds. *Collected articles from the Bulletin of the East Yorkshire Local History Society, nos. 1-55, 1970-Feb. 1997.* 2 vols. [ ]: the Society, 1997.

East Yorkshire Local History Society series. The Society, 1952- .

Halifax

Papers, reports, &c. read before the Halifax Antiquarian Society. 1902-28. Continued as *Transactions of the Halifax Antiquarian Society.* 1929- . Indexed in:

BRETTON, R. *Halifax Antiquarian Society. Index of transactions, titles & subjects, 1901-1941.* Halifax: Halifax Antiquarian Society, [1941].

Hull

The Local: newsletter of the Local History Unit, Hull College. 1986-94. Title varies. News, notes on new publications, *etc.*

Leeds

The publications of the Thoresby Society. Leeds: the Society, 1891- . Indexed in:

KIRK, GEORGE EDWARD. *Jubilee index to the publications of the Thoresby Society issued during the half century 1889-1939.* Leeds: Thoresby Society, 1941.

SINGLETON, JAMES. 'General index of the first six volumes of the *Miscellanea*', in *Miscellanea* [6]. *T.S.* 22, 1915, 409-21.

FORSTER, M. *Index to the publications of the Thoresby Society, volumes XXXVII-LI (1939-1968).* Supplement to *T.S.* 50. 1968.

Ryedale

The Ryedale historian. [ ]: Yorkshire Archaeological Society Helmsley and District Group, 1965- . (from 1972, published by Helmsley Archaeological Society).

Saddleworth

The bulletin of the Saddleworth Historical Society. 1971- .

Scarborough

The transactions of the Scarborough and District Archaeological Society. 1958-73.

Sheffield

Transactions of the Hunter Archaeological Society. Sheffield: J.W. Northend, 1914- .

Teesdale

Teesdale Record Society [proceedings]. 1935-46. Predominantly relating to Co. Durham, but includes some North Riding material.

Wakefield

Wakefield Historical Society journal. 1975- .

York

York historian. York: Yorkshire Architectural and York Archaeological Society, 1976- . Indexed in PEARSON, CHRISTINE. 'Index to York historian volumes 1-10', *York historian* 10, 1992, 82-115.

B. *Newspapers*

Newspapers contain a great deal of information of genealogical relevance – especially announcements of births, marriages, and deaths, but also advertisements and reports of current events. A number of listings of Yorkshire newspapers are available. *Newsplan* is a major attempt to list holdings of newspapers

in libraries nation-wide. A number of listings for Yorkshire have emanated from this project:

MELROSE, ELIZABETH ANNE, ed. *Newsplan in Yorkshire and Humberside cumulative update of local newspaper holdings in the Yorkshire and Humberside regions 1990-1995.* [ ]: Yorkshire & Humberside Newsplan, 1996.

PARKES, ANDREW. *Newsplan: report of the Newsplan project in Yorkshire and Humberside, March 1988-June, 1989.* British Library, 1990. Supplements, 1992 and 1993. Lists and locates newspapers.

Newsplan in Yorkshire & Humberside: index to local newspapers by place. Wakefield: Yorkshire & Humberside Newsplan Implementation Committee 1996.

A number of other listings are also availabe:

LAUGHTON, GEORGE E., & STEPHEN, LORNA R. *Yorkshire newspapers: a bibliography with locations.* Library Association Yorkshire Branch, 1960.

'Newspapers in Cleveland', *J.Cl.F.H.S.* 4(12), 1991, 8-11. List of newspapers in the libraries of Middlesbrough, Hartlepool, Redcar and Stockton.

'... Newspapers held at Skipton Reference Library', *K.D.F.H.S.J.* Winter 1998, 27. List.

MUNFORD, A.P. *South Yorkshire newspapers, 1754-1976.* Archive handlists 1. Barnsley: South Yorkshire County Council, Recreation Culture and Health Department, 1976. Lists 126 newspapers, with locations.

For indexes to the *Hull Advertiser* see:

MACMAHON, K.A. *An index to the more important local historical information contained in the files of the Hull Advertiser and Exchange Gazette.* Hull: [ ], 1955. Not seen. Covers 1794-1825.

PARRY, DAVID, ed. *The Meadley index to the Hull Advertiser.* 2 vols. Hull: Humberside College of Higher Education, 1987. v.1. 1826-1845. v.2. 1846-1857.

Family history societies and others have published a variety of extracts from old newspapers likely to be of genealogical interest. These include:

Bradford

KENZIE, K. 'From the front page of the *Chronicle and Mail, Bradford.* Wed., July 21, 1875', *Bod-kin* **19**, 1990, 12-14. Lists innumerable names, presumably from advertisements.

WALSH, JOSIE. 'The *Bradford Weekly Telegraph* pretty child competition', *Bodkin* **27**, 1992, 19; **28**, 1992, 16. List of children, October-December 1909.

Craven

'Obituaries from the *Craven household almanac*', *Wh.N.* **27-31**, 1998-9, *passim.* For 1901-4. Further obituaries presumably forthcoming.

MERRIDEW, STANLEY. 'Obituaries from the *Craven district household almanac*', *Wh.N.* **25**, 1997, 17-20. For 1928-9.

Doncaster

'Extract from the *Doncaster review*', *Don.Anc.* 3(4), 1987, 120-21. For June 1895.

Leeds

BROWN, JEAN, & JONES, BRIAN. *Yorkshire snippets.* 2 vols. Bradford: the authors, 1997. Personal notices, *etc.,* from the *Leeds mercury* and the *Bradford observer,* mainly 19th c.

'Leeds Mercury newspaper extracts from 1773-1774 inclusive', *H. & D.F.H.S.J.* 6(4), 1993, 139-42.

'Extracts from the *Leeds Mercury* newspaper Oct-Dec. 1787', *H. & D.F.H.S.J. passim.* Also from *Huddersfield Daily Examiner.* Death and other notices.

'Leeds Mercury newspaper extracts from January-August 1796', *H. & D.F.H.S.J.* 8(1), 1994, 31-4.

'Leeds Mercury newspaper extracts from January-December 1800', *H. & D.F.H.S.J.* 7(1), 1993, 31-4.

'Leeds Mercury newspaper: extracts from May-December 1808', *H. & D.F.H.S.J.* 6(3), 1993, 103-6. Legal notices, marriages, death notices, *etc.,* relating to the Huddersfield district.

'Leeds Mercury newspaper: extracts from January-April 1818', *H. & D.F.H.S.J.* 7(2), 1994, 63-6.

'Leeds Mercury newspaper: extracts from May-August 1818', *H. & D.F.H.S.J.* 7(3), 1994. 99-102.

'Leeds Mercury newspaper: extracts from September-December 1818', *H. & D.F.H.S.J.* 7(4), 1994, 135-8.

Ripon

'Entries in the *London gazette*', *R.H.* 1(1), 1988, 7-8. Relating to Ripon, later 17th c.

Sheffield

'Extracts from the *Sheffield register*', *F.S.* **2-4**, 1981-3. Deaths of prominent people recorded in the *Sheffield register,* published by the *Independent* newspaper. Mainly 18-19th c.

Rotherham

'The Rotherham *Advertiser*, July 1919: those taking part in the peace celebrations', *F.S.* 18(3), 1997, 96-9. List of names.

Shipley

WATSON, IAN. 'Inquests and obituaries: a selective list from the *Shipley and Saltaire Times,* 1876-1882', *Bod-kin* **26**, 1992, 8.

5. PLACE NAMES AND MAPS, etc.

A. Place Names

Obscure place-names frequently occur in genealogical sources, and it may on occasion prove difficult to locate them. A number of topographical dictionaries of Yorkshire were published in the eighteenth and nineteenth century; if you have access to any of these they may be of help:

CLARKE, STEPHEN REYNOLDS. *The new Yorkshire gazetteer or topographical dictionary.* Henry Teesdale and Co., 1828.

HARGROVE, ELY. *The Yorkshire gazetteer, or, a dictionary of the towns, villages and hamlets, monasteries and castles, principal mountains, rivers, &c., in the County of York, and Ainsty, or county of the City, of York, describing the situation of each, and the various events by which some of them have been distinguished.* 2nd ed. Knaresborough: Hargrave and Sons, 1812.

LANGDALE, THOMAS. *A topographical dictionary of Yorkshire, containing the names of all the towns, villages, hamlets, gentlemen's seats, &c., in the County of York, alphabetically arranged under the heads of the North, East and West Ridings, also in what parish, township, wapentake, division and liberty they are situated ...* 2nd ed. Northallerton: J. Langdale, 1822.

Nomina villarum Eboracensium, or, an index of all the towns and villages in the County of York and County of the City of York, alphabetically digested, shewing at one view within what Riding, wapentake and liberty each town and village is situate; also the borough towns, parishes and chapelries, and the market towns, with the market and fair days; also containing the names of all the lords and chief bailiffs of liberties, with the proper directions to them of warrants on writs, together with the names and places of abode of all the chief constables of wapontakes and liberties, coroners and bailiffs within the County of York. York: A. Ward, 1768.

Genealogical sources do not, of course, always spell place-names as we would. Texts from earlier centuries may give quite different spellings from those we are used to. The study of place names and their origins and their etymology, may be helpful in determining locations. There are two general studies of Yorkshire place-names:

MORRIS, W. *Yorkshire through place names.* Newton Abbot: David & Charles, 1982.

THURLOW, WILLIAM. *Yorkshire place-names.* Clapham: Dalesman, 1979.

There are also a number of place-name dictionaries. For Domesday place names, see:

TURNER, J.H. *Yorkshire place names, as recorded in the Yorkshire Domesday Book, 1086 ...* Bingley: the author, [1909].

A number of etymological dictionaries for specific Ridings are also available; these show many variations in spelling since names were first written down. The titles published by the English Place Name Society are authoritative and widely available.

East Riding

SMITH, A.H. *The place-names of the East Riding of Yorkshire and York.* English Place-Name Society **14**. 1937.

NICHOLSON, JOHN. 'Place-names of the East Riding of Yorkshire', *T.E.R.A.S.* **25**, 1926, 1-137. Etymological dictionary.

North Riding

SMITH, A.H. *The place-names of the North Riding of Yorkshire.* English Place-Name Society **5**. 1928.

West Riding

SMITH, A.H. *The place-names of the West Riding of Yorkshire.* 8 vols. English Place-Name Society **30-37**. 1961-63. Pt.1. Lower and Upper Strafforth and Staincross Wapentakes; Pt.2. Osgoldcross and Agbrigg Wapentakes; Pt.3. Morley Wapentake; Pt.4. Barkston Ash, Skyrack and Ainsty Wapentakes; Pt.5. Upper and Lower Claro Wapentakes; Pt.6. East and West Staincliffe and Ewcross Wapentakes; Pt.7. Introduction, bibliography, river-names, analyses; Pt.8. Index of West Riding place-names (incorporating the East and North Ridings).

MOORMAN, F.W. *The place-names of the West Riding of Yorkshire.* T.S. **18**. 1910.

B. Maps and Atlases

Maps of parish boundaries are of particular value for genealogists, since they identify the parishes between which ancesters could have moved most easily. Every Yorkshire genealogist should consult:

HARVEY, J.H. *Yorkshire ancient parishes and archdeaconries; based on George Lawton's collections relative to York and Ripon (1842) & Henry Teesdale's map of Yorkshire (1817-1828)*. Leeds: Y.A.S., P.R.S., 1973. Sheet map.

This map may be complemented by the listings of contiguous parishes published by CART Publications:

East Riding contiguous parishes. CART Publications, 1997.

North Riding contiguous parishes. CART Publications, 1997.

West Riding contiguous parishes. CART Publications, 1997.

On Yorkshire maps in general, see:

RAISTRICK, A. *Yorkshire maps and map-makers*. Clapham: Dalesman, 1969. General discussion.

RAWNSLEY, JOHN E. *Antique maps of Yorkshire and their makers*. Guiseley: [the author], 1970. Brief biographies of cartographers.

The history of Yorkshire is mapped in:

NEAVE, SUSAN, & ELLIS, STEPHEN. *An historical atlas of East Yorkshire*. Hull: University of Hull Press, 1996.

Old maps of the county are listed in:

WHITAKER, HAROLD. *A descriptive list of the printed maps of Yorkshire and its Ridings, 1577-1900*. Y.A.S., R.S. **86**. 1933.

A number of record offices have published catalogues of the maps in their care – both printed and manuscript. Estate maps may be particularly useful if they include names of tenants. For tithe maps and apportionments see the section on them in volume 4 of *Yorkshire: the genealogists library guide*.

KIRK, G.E. *Catalogue of the maps and plans in the library of the Yorkshire Archaeological Society ...* [Leeds]: the Society, 1937.

CURR, ISHBEL. 'A collection of maps and plans in the Archives Department of Cleveland County Libraries', *C.T.L.H.S.B.* **33**, 1977, 32-4. Descriptive account.

DYSON, BRIAN. *Yorkshire maps and plans in the archives of the University of Hull*. Sources for regional and local history **4**. Hull: Centre for Regional & Local History, University of Hull, 1990.

List of North Yorkshire and North Riding maps & plans available for consultation in the North Yorkshire County Record Office. Guide **3**. Northallerton: North Yorkshire County Record Office, 1990.

A guide to the Fairbank collection of maps, plans and surveyors' books and correspondence in the Reference Library. Sheffield: Sheffield City Libraries, 1936. Collection of a firm of surveyors business archive, which includes numerous plans and field books naming owners, *etc.*, 18-19th c. See also:

HALL, THOMAS WALTER. *The Fairbanks of Sheffield 1688-1848*. Sheffield: N.W. Northend, 1932. Facsimiles of surveys from the Fairbank collections: includes the names of some landowners. Also includes brief pedigree of Fairbanks, 18-19th c. 'The Fairbank collection', *T. Hunter A.S.* **4**, 1937, 172-4.

For a modern reproduction of an eighteenth-century map, see:

JEFFERYS, THOMAS. *The County of York survey'd, 1775*. Menston: Scholar Press, 1971. Not seen.

Early editions of Ordnance Survey maps are particularly useful for genealogists, since they provide considerable detail of how the landscape appeared to our ancestors before the huge changes of the last century or so. Two facsimile editions have been published in book form:

BRUFF, BARRY, ed. *The village atlas: the growth of North and West Yorkshire, 1840-1910*. Village Press, 1990. Reprint of the first three editions of the Ordnance Survey maps.

The old series Ordnance Survey maps of England and Wales ... 8 vols. Lympne Castle: Harry Margary, 1981-91. Yorkshire is covered in vols.5, Lincolnshire, Rutland and East Anglia, 7, North-Central England and 8, Northern England and the Isle of Man. Individual Ordnance Survey sheet maps have also been reprinted by the publisher David & Charles.

Barnsley

'County Borough of Barnsley: map of Barnsley A.D. 1777', *J. Barnsley F.H.S.* 3(4), 1995, 22-6. Lists names of residents or owners.

Leeds

BONSER, KENNETH J., & NICHOLS, HAROLD. *Printed maps and plans of Leeds, 1711-1900.* T.S. **47**. 1960.

Sheffield

'Changes in Sheffield street names', *F.S.* 3(3), 1982, 63-4. List of changes made, c.1871.

7. MIGRATION

A. *Immigration*

The movement of people creates major difficulties for the genealogist. Studies of migration may sometimes offer clues as to where ancestors came from. There are a number of studies of migration to specific places in Yorkshire; these are listed here.

Bradford

ARONSFELD, C.C. 'German Jews in nineteenth century Bradford', *Y.A.J.* **53**, 1981, 111-17.

Carlton

JONES, MELVYN. 'Long-distance migrants and cultural identity: the example of a Welsh colony in South Yorkshire', *Local historian* **26**(4), 1996, 223-36. Study of migrants from Mostyn, Flintshire to Carlton, late 19th c.

Darfield

WALKER, A.G. 'Migration into a South Yorkshire colliery district, 1861-1881', *N.H.* **29**, 1993, 165-84. Study of Darfield census returns.

Hull

NEAVE, DAVID. *The Dutch connection: the Anglo-Dutch heritage of Hull and Humberside.* Hull: Humberside Leisure Services, 1988. Brief general study.
WOODHOUSE, D.G. *Anti-German sentiment in Kingston-upon-Hull: the German community and the First World War.* Hull: Kingston-upon-Hull City Record Office, 1990. Includes list of persons and properties attached, with some names.

Leeds

BUCKMAN, JOSEPH. *Immigrants and the class struggle: the Jewish immigrant in Leeds, 1880-1914.* Manchester: Manchester University Press, 1983. General study; few names.

Middlesbrough

GWYNNE, TERENCE, & SILL, MICHAEL. 'Welsh immigration into Middlesbrough in the mid-nineteenth century', *C.T.L.H.S.B.* **31**, 1976, 19-22. Brief discussion.

Sheffield

AWTY, BRIAN G. 'French immigrants and the iron industry in Sheffield', *Y.A.J.* **53**, 1981, 57-62. Based partly on parish registers.

York

FINNEGAN, FRANCES. *Poverty and prejudice: a study of Irish immigrants in York, 1840-1875.* Cork: Cork University Press, 1982.

PALLISER, D.M. 'A regional capital as magnet: immigrants to York, 1477-1566', *Y.A.J.* **57**, 1985, 111-23.

B. Emigration

For Yorkshire-born lord mayors of London, see:

TAYLOR, R.V. 'Yorkshire Lord mayors of London', *Y.N.Q.II.* **1**, 1905, 148-50.

'Yorkshire Lord mayors of London', *Y.C.M.* **1**, 1891, 205-8. List of 21 mayors, with brief biographical notes.

North America

There are two substantial lists of Yorkshire felons transported to North America:

PERRY, J. 'The transportation of felons to America, 1717-1775: some North Riding quarter sessions records, 1717-1775', *Journal* **8**; N.Y.C.R.O.P. **27**, 1981, 65-117. Includes list of persons transported.

Transportation from Hull and the East Riding to America & Australia, taken from Quarter Sessions records. Hull: E.Y.F.H.S., 1984. Lists transportees, 1707-1856.

Other works on emigration to North America include (in rough chronological order):

MORRIS, G.E., & GREENE, FRANCIS THORNTON. 'North Riding emigration and the first families of Virginia', *Ryedale historian* **14**, 1988-9, 39-41. Includes list of Virginian families from the North Riding.

MCLEE, C. 'Yorkshire emigrants to the west, 1773-1776', *Cl.F.H.S.J.* **4**(1), 1989, 37-40. List of emigrants to North America.

HENNESSEY, G.P. 'The Yorkshire migration', *F.S.* **9**(2), 1988, 40-42; **9**(3), 1988, 67-8. List of passengers on the *Albion* and the *Jenny,* migrants from Hull to Fort Cumberland, Canada, 1774-5.

PIPES, JACQUI. 'Yorkshire emigrants ... ,' *J.Cl.F.H.S.* **4**(3), 1989, 38-40. List of Yorkshire passengers who sailed from Hull to Nova Scotia, 1774.

HYSLOP, JAYNE. 'Yorkshire ancestors in Canada', *J.Cl.F.H.S.* **5**(5), 1993, 29-32. List of Yorkshire emigrants in New York wishing to relocate to Nova Scotia, 1817.

MCMASTER, ANNE. 'From the *Montreal transcript*', *Y.F.H.* **13**(3), 1987, 59. List of Yorkshire people killed and wounded when the schooner *Shamrock* blew up on its way from Montreal to Kingston, 9 July 1842.

Australia

For an important list of transportees to Australia, see above under North America. Other works on emigration to Australia include (in rough chronological order):

'The second fleet: Britain's grim convict armada of 1790', *J. Barnsley F.H.S.* **4**(1), 1996, 13-16. Brief biographical notes on Yorkshire transportees to Australia.

'Sydney Cove chronicle, 30th June 1790. At last the transports are here. 278 died on the fearsome journey to Sydney Cove', *J.Cl.F.H.S.* **3**(10), 1988, 12-13. Includes list of transportees from Yorkshire and other northern counties.

'Australian cops and robbers', *B.T.* **46**, 1991, 26. List of Yorkshire prisoners discharged in Victoria in 1884.

DENNIS, EDNA. 'Coroners' inquests, N.S. Wales, Australia: entries from the index & registers of coroners' inquests, 1914-1920', *Y.F.H.* **20**(6), 1994, 141-3. Relating to Yorkshire-born emigrants.

Author Index

Family Name Index

Place Name Index